Annotated Legal Documents on Islam in Europe: The Netherlands

Annotated Legal Documents on Islam in Europe

VOLUME 4

The titles published in this series are listed at *brill.com/ldie*

Annotated Legal Documents on Islam in Europe:

The Netherlands

Compiled and Annotated by

Agnieszka Szumigalska

BRILL

LEIDEN | BOSTON

Library of Congress Cataloging-in-Publication Data

Szumigalska, Agnieszka.
Annotated legal documents on Islam in Europe. the Netherlands / compiled and annotated by Agnieszka Szumigalska.
pages cm. – (Annotated legal documents on Islam in Europe, ISSN 2214-1340 ; volume 4)
Includes bibliographical references and index.
ISBN 978-90-04-29017-4 (pbk. : alk. paper) 1. Muslims–Legal status, laws, etc.–Netherlands. I. Title.

KKM2467.M56S98 2015
342.49208'5297–dc23

2014047374

This publication has been typeset in the multilingual "Brill" typeface. With over 5,100 characters covering Latin, IPA, Greek, and Cyrillic, this typeface is especially suitable for use in the humanities. For more information, please see www.brill.com/brill-typeface.

ISSN 2214-1340
ISBN 978-90-04-29017-4 (paperback)

This book is printed on acid-free paper.

FSC www.fsc.org MIX Paper from responsible sources FSC® C109576

Printed by Printforce, the Netherlands

Contents

Foreword by the Editors

This is the fourth volume in the new series *Annotated Legal Documents on Islam in Europe*. The publication of this series reflects the growing concern with the status of Islam in Europe which has been expressed in recent years. This has most obviously been the case in political discourse, something which can be traced back to the early 1990s. But the concern has also moved into the legal field, most markedly, of course, with limitations on Muslim female dress enacted in France and Belgium and the ban on building minarets on mosques in Switzerland. The discussions provoked by these events have often reflected a general ignorance about the religious status and rights of Muslims in the various European countries, status and rights which can differ significantly. A closer look at the legislation quickly shows how different it can be from one country to another and, in some cases, how far back in time such legislation can go. Despite the common legal and political foundations constructed since 1945 in instruments such as the European Convention on Human Rights and the more recently accumulated legislation of the European Union, this closer look reveals how difficult it can be to talk of the 'European practice' in this field. In some countries Islam has an officially recognised status which in several cases originates in the first half of the 20th century, so is not new. In other countries no such recognition of any religion is available even if informal ways of favouring one religion over another may exist. Since 1990 especially, European courts have moved to equalise the status of Islam with that of other religions in the practical exercise of religious freedom in various countries. Particular practices regarded as core religious obligations—in the case of Islam practices such as male circumcision, access to correctly slaughtered meat and otherwise *halal* food, free time for the main periods of worship and religious festivals, and the right to build mosques—can be controversial in some countries while less so in others. Children's access to Islamic religious instruction can be achieved in cooperation with the state education systems in some countries, while in others the community must rely on its own arrangements. All of these multitudinous issues are reflected variously in the national legislation.

The aim of this series is to make this legislation available to both the interested researcher and the practising lawyer. Altogether the series is expected to comprise 32 volumes, one for each of the 28 countries of the European Union plus Norway and Switzerland, and a volume each dealing with the European Union (treaties, directives and decisions of the Court of Justice of the European Communities) and the European Court of Human Rights. Excerpts of relevant legislation will be introduced and summarised by the volume compiler, and where court cases have provided significant interpretation of the law they will also be referred to. The legislation itself is reproduced in the original language, as the editors and the publisher agreed early on in the preparation of the series that any attempt to translate legislation into English would be unsatisfactory and could be misleading. The annotation by the compiler should give sufficient guidance to users to allow a decision as to whether to arrange a translation for their specific purposes.

While there is in many countries legislation explicitly referring to aspects of Islam, most often regarding official recognition or to do with education, in other countries there is none—the Netherlands has been moving towards the latter category. At first glance this volume will therefore appear to be a presentation of the status of religions generally. But the compiler's annotations and references to case law, as well as to the implications of relevant elements of the system of 'pillarisation' (*verzuiling*) which has only recently been set aside, will in most instances indicate how such general legislation can apply to Islam in practice.

An attempt has been made to ensure that the volumes are structured in as similar a manner as possible. The starting point for this has been the thematic organisation of the *Yearbook of Muslims in Europe* which Brill has published annually since 2009. But it has only been a starting point, and in each volume the compiler and the editors have agreed on the structure which makes most sense for the legislation of the country concerned. One member of the editorial group has taken responsibility for discussing the structure and compilation of each volume. We are grateful to Kate Elliott for the care shown in copy editing the volume. The idea for this project came from the publisher, where Nicolette van der Hoek and Nienke Brienen-Moolenaar have played an invaluable role in ensuring that the project has got off the ground. Editors appreciate how much their expertise contributes to ensuring that a project like this can run smoothly.

It is in the nature of such a project that each volume, if left as it stands, will gradually become out of date as new legislation and cases appear. It is the intention of the editors and publishers in due course to make the contents available on-line in a form which will permit regular updating.

The Editors
October 2014

General Introduction

Relations between the state and church(es) have played a significant role in Dutch history. For a very long period of time (since its appearance in the 4th–6th century[1]), Christianity formed the dominant religious power in that part of Europe. One may state that Christianity's strong position both set the tone of public debate in the Netherlands and, as a result, contributed to particular political solutions. Interestingly enough, whereas e.g. in the 17th century the establishment of state churches was a common and widely acknowledged practice in Europe, the Republic of the United Netherlands never went that far in church-state policy.[2] This illustrates the Dutch concept of religious freedom and church-state relations. For a long period of time, the position of Protestantism was privileged in the public sphere but membership of the church was not compulsory.[3]

Religious (primarily Catholic *versus* Protestant) affiliation historically formed one of the crucial foundations of Dutch identity. The delineation between Catholicism and Protestantism (and the rest of Dutch society marked by more liberal attitudes) led to deep socio-political cleavages, which found their culmination in the 19th century system of social pillars.[4] The process of

1 Trouillez, Pierre, 'De eerste kerstening van de Lage Landen. Een verhaal van slagen en falen …' in *Geloven in de Lage Landen. Scharniermomenten in de geschiedenis van het christendom*, Peter Nissen (Leuven: Davidsfonds 2004), pp. 9–15. First, the south of the Netherlands was Christianised, while in the North the process took much longer. See Nissen, Peter, 'De moeizame kerstening van het noorden' in *Geloven in de Lage Landen* …, Nissen, pp. 27–28.

2 The Dutch Reformed Church (*Gereformeerde Kerk*, later also *Nederlandse Hervormde Kerk*), which consequently reinforced and confirmed its profound socio-political position in the Netherlands, was a "public church". See Snel, Jan D., "Het misverstand over kerk en staat", *Trouw*, 13 March 2004, available at http://www.trouw.nl/tr/nl/4324/Nieuws/archief/article/detail/1760359/2004/03/13/Het-misverstand-over-kerk-en-staat.dhtml [last accessed on 10 december 2014].

3 See Snel, "Het misverstand over kerk en staat".

4 The Dutch pillar-based society was divided into three or, according to some authors, four vertical "segments", i.e. Protestants, Catholics, liberals and, alternatively, socialists. The system of social pillars has been broadly discussed in scholarly literature. See e.g. Lijphart, Arend, *The Politics of Accommodation: Pluralism and Democracy in the Netherlands* (Berkeley: University of California Press, 1968); Spiecker, Ben, Steutel, Jan, 'Multiculturalism, Pillarization and Liberal Civic Education in The Netherlands', *International Journal of Educational Research*, 35 (2001), pp. 293–304; Post, Harry, Pillarization: An Analysis of Dutch and Belgian Society (Aldershot etc.: Avebury, 1989); Hellemans, Staf, *Strijd om de moderniteit: sociale bewegingen*

pillarisation (i.e. the formation of social vertical structures) spanned all paths of socio-political life (from cultural activities, e.g. the system of media and sports clubs, to trade unions and insurance associations, to political parties), contributing to a certain mutual isolation of particular communities. In this regard, a special role was played by the education issue. One should note that the contemporary system of education in the Netherlands is still influenced by the tradition of social pillars. The solutions adopted in this regard were later also extended to other, i.e. non-Christian (including Islamic) denominations.[5]

In the 1960s, the system of depillarisation (i.e. the erosion of social pillars) led to the fundamental restructuring of Dutch society. These somewhat revolutionary developments were accompanied by the processes of secularization, liberalization and increasing emancipation of Dutch society. At the same time the first symptoms of further cultural (including religious) changes were becoming increasingly visible. One may state that the contemporary Dutch concept of church-state relations and, in a broader sense, the idea of social culture find their origin in two key elements. The first includes the aforementioned tradition of pillarisation, while the second factor refers to the 'polder model' (*poldermodel*) which embodies the Dutch negotiable style of policy-making. When considering Dutch modern history, one should also emphasise the post-war developments which resulted in the deepening cultural and religious diversification of Dutch society. In this regard, particular attention is paid to the appearance of Islamic immigrants in the Netherlands and their activity.

The presence of Islam in Dutch culture is 'a result of large-scale immigration',[6] which has determined the complex ethno-religious character of Islamic minorities. The presence of Islam in the Netherlands has become visible since the mid-20th century. In the 1950s and 1960s large groups of Moluccan and Suri-

---

en verzuiling in Europa sinds 1800 (Leuven: Universitaire Pres Leuven, 1990); Stuurman, Siep, *Verzuiling, kapitalisme en patriarchaat* (Nijmegen: SUN, 1983); Karsten, Sjoerd, 'Verzuiling als sociaal en politiek verschijnsel' in *Verzuiling in het onderwijs. Actuele verklaringen en analyse*, Anne B. Dijkstra, Jaap Dronkers, Roeland Hofman (eds.) (Groningen: Wolters-Noordhoff Groningen, 1997); Kruijt, Jakob P., Goddijn, Walter, *Verzuiling en koninklijke ontzuiling als sociologisch proces*, in *Drift en koers*, Arie Nicolaas Jan den Hollander et al. (eds.) (Assen: Drukkerij Van Gorcum & Comp., 1968).

5 See Chapter 7.

6 Sunier, Thijl, 'Islam in the Netherlands. A nation despite religious communities?' in *Religious Newcomers and the Nation State. Political Culture and Organized Religion in France and the Netherlands*, Erik Sengers, Thijl Sunier (eds.) (Delft: Eburon, 2010), p. 115.

namese Muslims,[7] as well as Muslims from Turkey and North Africa, began to appear in the Netherlands.[8] Initially, these groups were perceived in terms of a temporary stay (for labour purposes), which resulted in virtually no attention being paid to the religious aspects of their activity. The policy of family reunion was one of the main factors that led to the shift from a temporary to a permanent stay,[9] contributing to a change in the way Islamic immigrants were perceived in the Netherlands. With regard to that period, one should also note the presence of immigrants (asylum seekers in particular) from Iraq, Somalia, Ghana and former Yugoslavia.[10] Hence, it should be emphasised that Muslims have not formed a cohesive community in the Netherlands but, on the contrary, they hail from various ethno-cultural and religious backgrounds and traditions. Moreover, the levels of religiosity and religious involvement of particular ethnic groups also vary.[11]

Since the 1970s, the process of the institutionalisation of Islamic (primarily Turkish and Moroccan) groups in the Netherlands has been notable. Simultaneously, Muslims began to organise their place in Dutch society with special attention being devoted to cultural and religious aspects. As a result, the first political claims were formed with regard to issues such as e.g. the existence and conditions of the establishment of Islamic prayer houses and mosques. In 1955 the first mosque was built in the Netherlands (in the Hague[12]), and in 1975 the first mosque with financial support from the state was established. Very soon other steps were made, such as e.g. the enactment of regulations concerning

7 One should note that although indeed the first Islamic groups came from the Dutch former colonies (Indonesia, subsequently also Suriname and the Netherlands Antilles), those groups do not make up the majority of Muslims in the Netherlands. Sunier, 'Islam in the Netherlands ...', p. 115.

8 Rath, Jan, Penninx, Rinus, Groenendijk, Kees, Meijer, Astrid, *Nederland en zijn Islam. Een ontzuilende samenleving reageert op het onstaat van een geloofgemeenschap* (Amsterdam: Het Spinhuis, 1996), pp. 3–4.

9 Rath, Penninx, Groenendijk, Meijer, *Nederland en zijn Islam ...*, pp. 4–5; Sunier, 'Islam in the Netherlands ...', pp. 115–116 and 121.

10 These groups were formed mainly by asylum-seekers. See e.g. Loenen, Titia, *Geloof in het geding. Juridische grenzen van religious pluralisme in het perspectief van de mensenrechten*. Infoplus Minderheden (The Hague: Sdu Uitgevers, 2006), p. 9.

11 See Maliepaard, Mieke, Gijsberts, Mérove, *Moslim in Nederland*, Sociaal en Cultureel Planbureau (The Hague: 2012), available at www.ru.nl/publish/pages/671794/moslim_in _nederland_1.pdf, pp. 14–15.

12 Bernts, Ton, Jong de, Gert. Yar, Hasan, 'Een religieuze atlas van Nederland' in *Geloven in het publieke domein. Verkenningen van een dubbele transformatie*, Wim B.H.J. van de Donk et. al. (Amsterdam: Amsterdam University Press, 2006), p. 113.

Islamic cemeteries, chaplaincy, media, the ritual slaughter of animals and education (the main postulate pertained to the right to establish Islamic schools within the framework of the existing system of education). Aside from the formal, institutional realm, Dutch Muslims began to organise their presence and activities in other socio-cultural dimensions.[13]

In the 1980s the first political concepts of the integration of (Islamic) immigrants within Dutch society were formulated and discussed. The main idea was based on the balance between Muslims' participation in Dutch society and respect for Islamic culture, identities and traditions. In the 1980s and 1990s the Islamic issue became one of the crucial, broadly discussed topics in the Dutch political arena, with special emphasis being placed on the need for Muslims' participation in the fields of labour, housing and education.[14] The discussion involved certain political arrangements aimed at the further integration of Muslims (in both cultural and economic terms). At the same time, the discourse was to a certain extent marked by social fears and distrust of Islamic—'foreign'—culture. Social attitudes towards Islam, and its reception in the whole of Europe, including the Netherlands, have additionally been influenced by the events of 11 September 2001.[15]

According to the survey conducted by the Central Bureau of Statistics—Statistics Netherlands (*Centraal Bureau voor de Statistiek, CBS*) in 2008, approximately 825,000 Muslims live in the Netherlands, making up 5 per cent of Dutch society. Two-thirds of Muslims are of Moroccan or Turkish origin (according to data from 2009—296,000 and 285,000, respectively). Other large groups are primarily formed by Muslims from Suriname, Afghanistan, Iraq, Somalia and Iran.[16]

The Constitution is the highest legal act in Dutch legislation. Several constitutional provisions guarantee the fulfilment of the principles of equality and freedom in a broad sense. Additionally, in legislative practice a number of legal acts may refer to Islamic issues. It may be noted that since the 1990s many relevant acts have been introduced which (directly or indirectly) refer to Islamic communities (e.g. regulations concerning ritual slaughtering of animals, integration law, work conditions, non-discrimination policy), while more general legislative foundations were established in earlier periods (e.g. with regard to

13 See Rath, Penninx, Groenendijk, Meijer, *Nederland en zijn Islam …*, pp. 4–5; Sunier, 'Islam in the Netherlands …', pp. 115–116 and 121.

14 Sunier, 'Islam in the Netherlands …', p. 122.

15 Sunier, 'Islam in the Netherlands …', pp. 125–127.

16 Maliepaard, Gijsberts, *Moslim in Nederland*, pp. 44–45. See also Chapter 2.

the system of education, freedom of religion etc.). Moreover, a significant role in the interpretation of law has been played by Dutch jurisprudence.

This volume focuses on the analysis of national legal conditions regarding the presence and activity of Muslims in the Netherlands. Each chapter begins with a brief introduction presenting the relevant legal regulations and/or background information concerning social, political or historical factors which contributed to their enactment. Wherever it was possible, selected examples of relevant Dutch jurisprudence have also been referred to in order to illustrate the judicial interpretation of particular legal issues in practice. Regarding the Dutch system of law, the main electronic sources used in this volume are www.wetten.overheid.nl (an updated database of Dutch legislation) and www.wetboek-online.nl. Full texts of the examples of Dutch jurisprudence chosen may be found, as regards the most recent cases, on www.rechtspraak.nl. The information included in this volume was last updated in June 2014.

CHAPTER 1

Status of Religious Communities

1.1 Constitutional Guarantees

The relations between the state and religion have been broadly debated throughout Dutch history, resulting in a range of legislative (including constitutional) developments.[1] The current Constitution of the Kingdom of the Netherlands (Grondwet voor het Koninkrijk der Nederlanden) came into force on 17 February 1983 and was preceded by a long debate in which worldview issues and cultural visions of Dutch society played a relevant role.

The work aimed at creating the new constitution was initiated in the period marked by the still relatively strong influence of social pillars. This factor was paralleled by the fact that it was not until the second half of the 20th century that the presence and activity of Muslims became noticeable. These developments considerably contributed to the shape of the Constitution. The legislative approach towards religious communities at the time was primarily Christian-centred as regards the terminology of churches and religious practices. Nevertheless, the second half of the 20th century saw not only the increasing relevance of non-Christian groups ('newcomers') in Dutch society, but also processes leading to the erosion of the system of social pillars ('depillarisation'), socio-cultural emancipation and secularisation. These factors considerably influenced the direction of further legislative developments in the Netherlands.

The establishment of the new Constitution was preceded by broad legislative consultation (including consideration of the relevant international regulations, particularly Art. 9 of the European Convention on Human Rights) and the involvement of social groups.[2] During the creation of the new constitution,

1 Here, the constitutional developments since the mid 19th century are worth special attention (e.g. the Constitution of 1848) with regard to the interpretation of religious freedom and the separation of church and state. The overview of Dutch historical constitutions is available at http://www.denederlandsegrondwet.nl/9353000/1/j9vvihlf299q0sr/vidyfoke5w7x [last accessed on 30 November 2013].

2 Labuschagne, Barend Christoffel, *Godsdienstvrijheid en niet-gevestigde religies. Een grondrechtelijk-rechtsfilosofische studie naar de betekenis en grenzen van religieuze tolerantie* (Groningen: Wolters-Noordhoff, 1994), p. 73. In 1963 a special working group 'Proeve van een nieuwe grondwet' was established with the main purpose of analysing and proposing constitutional

special attention was paid to the tenets of 'freedom' and the definition of 'churches' (which were commonly interpreted as referring primarily, if not exclusively, to Christian denominations). Two state commissions (Van Schaik and Staatscommissie Cals-Donner) were formed to scrutinise the terminological aspects with respect to the post-war developments in the country. The 1983 Constitution was established as result of their work and assessments.

The Dutch Constitution of 1983 (including subsequent amendments) refers to the principles of religious freedom and equality in a relatively brief manner and does not explicitly refer to any particular denomination, nor does it refer to any category of religious organisation, community or church. Classic fundamental rights have been included in Title 1. The concepts of state neutrality, the notions of a secular state and the separation of church and state have not been defined. It appears that in the Dutch case these tenets are being shaped in socio-political and legal practice, as well as secondary legislation. Moreover, one should note that the hierarchy and mutual relations between fundamental rights and freedoms (including e.g. the freedom of religion) have not been defined in the Constitution. Due to the lack of precise provisions regarding religious freedom, as well as individual and collective rights concerning religious practices, a range of other legal guarantees have been introduced (e.g. the 1994 Common Equal Treatment Act—Algemene Wet Gelijke Behandeling[3]). In the event of any disputes requiring legal adjudication, a significant role is played by legal interpretation (as well as the advice or decisions of other legitimised institutions, advisory bodies and commissions) and court judgments.[4]

The Constitution of 1983 guarantees the freedom of religion and worldview. The text encompasses the terms of (religious) beliefs in a relatively broad and general manner, particularly in comparison to the Constitution of 1953,[5] in which 'religion' was assigned the whole of Chapter 5. Moreover, along with

---

developments. One of the elements under scrutiny was the shape of constitutional guarantees of religious freedom. Moreover, the report also included recommendations for the abolition of state funded clergy. See Labuschagne, *Godsdienstvrijheid* ..., pp. 73–74 and Bijsterveld, Sophie C. van, *Godsdienstvrijheid in Europees perspectief* (Deventer: W.E.J. Tjeenk Willink, 1998), pp. 78–79.

3 See more in Chapters 11 and 14.

4 See Gerards, Janneke H., 'Botsende grondrechten, het gelijkheidsbeginsel en belangenafwegingen door de rechter', in *Moderne gelijkheid. Lezingen, gehouden tijdens de Rechten van de mens-dag van de Erasmus Universiteit Rotterdam op 10 december 2004*, Janneke H. Gerards, Siep Stuurman, (Den Haag: Boom Juridische uitgevers, 2005), pp. 21–31.

5 The text of the Constitution of 1953 is available at http://www.denederlandsegrondwet.nl/9353000/1/j9vvihlf299q0sr/vi7lectkacu3 [last accessed on 25 January 2014].

religion, Art. 1 also includes the notion of a worldview (*levensovertuiging*, literally 'philosophy of life')—the solution recommended by the Van Schaik State Commission. Nevertheless, in the opinion of some authors, the Constitution precisely defines neither 'belief' nor 'worldview', e.g. in the context of manifesting one's religious convictions. The Constitution does not stipulate whether this freedom is limited by an ecclesiastical building's walls, nor does it give any definition of religious practices. Any limitations to fundamental laws may be introduced via the requirement of an Act of Parliament on the subject, which is a relatively restrictive principle.[6] One may conclude that this regulation is aimed at guaranteeing that no such restrictions may be imposed without deep-grounded justification.

The constitutional principle of the freedom of religion (and worldview) is deeply rooted in a broad legislative context, i.e. it has been embraced by a range of legal regulations, which refer to religious issues in an implicit rather than an explicit manner. This principle is indirectly related to the constitutionally defined categories of freedom, i.e. the freedom of the media (Art. 7), association (Art. 8),[7] assembly and demonstration (Art. 9).[8] The constitutionally guaranteed freedom is not absolute—the expression of convictions and beliefs in public is at one's discretion.[9] This responsibility refers to circumstances exceeding the acknowledged boundaries (i.e. the conditions of public order). This broad and rather vague term leaves room for legal interpretations of the rule, and also requires the involvement of other competent bodies.[10]

---

6 See e.g. Dekker—van Bijsterveld, Sophie C. den, *De verhouding tussen kerk en staat in het licht van de grondrechten* (Zwolle: W.E.J. Tjeenk Willink, 1988), pp. 51–52.

7 The freedom of association, as stipulated in Art. 8, is recognised in Dutch law, with possible restrictions applicable in cases when a breach of the peace is committed. This law also refers to the right to organise and attend meetings, gatherings and assemblies of a religious character.

8 In Art. 9, the right to organise demonstrations has been guaranteed, and this may be extended to religious demonstrations. This right may nevertheless be restricted if it can be justified by the rules of public order.

9 See Janssens, Alfred L.J., Nieuwenhuis, Aernout J., *Uitingsdelicten* (Deventer: Kluwer, 2005), p. 23.

10 Here, one should note that Dutch courts are not competent to judge the conjunction of legal acts with the Dutch Constitution, as stipulated in Art. 120 of the Constitution. Nevertheless, the courts can analyse their conformity with other legal Acts, e.g. the AWGB and international regulations—see Loenen, Titia, *Geloof in het geding: juridische grenzen van religieus pluralisme in het perspectief van de mensenrechten* (Den Haag: SDU, 2006), p. 20.

Another constitutional provision which indirectly touches on the rights and freedoms of Muslims in the Netherlands is the right to the inviolability of one's body, included in Art. 11 of the Constitution. Hereby, one may refer to the male circumcision issue, which forms an element of Islamic tradition. Nevertheless, the commonly applied legal interpretation of this provision leaves room for the practising of male circumcision in accordance with one's religious traditions.[11]

The key constitutional provisions referring to the freedom of religion have been included in Art. 6, which encompasses freedom both in its individual and collective dimensions (Art. 6.1). The limits of religious freedom have been defined by the system of law, based on the principle of each person's equality before the law. Moreover, both 'internal' (i.e. the right to *have* convictions) and 'external' (i.e. the *manifestation* of convictions and religious practices) aspects of freedom have been included. The 'external' dimension of religious freedom, as stipulated in Art. 6.2, can be further defined (and confined) in Dutch law. As referred to previously, possible restrictions may be justified by the rules of public order.

Grondwet voor het Koninkrijk der Nederlanden, 17 February 1983[12]

Artikel 1
Allen die zich in Nederland bevinden, worden in gelijke gevallen gelijk behandeld. Discriminatie wegens godsdienst, levensovertuiging, politieke gezindheid, ras, geslacht of op welke grond dan ook, is niet toegestaan.
[...]

Artikel 6
1. Ieder heeft het recht zijn godsdienst of levensovertuiging, individueel of in gemeenschap met anderen, vrij te belijden, behoudens ieders verantwoordelijkheid volgens de wet.
2. De wet kan ter zake van de uitoefening van dit recht buiten gebouwen en besloten plaatsen regels stellen ter bescherming van de gezondheid, in het belang van het verkeer en ter bestrijding of voorkoming van wanordelijkheden.

11 See more in section 15.3.

12 Grondwet voor het Koninkrijk der Nederlanden, available at http://wetten.overheid.nl/BWBR0001840 [last accessed on 2 June 2014]. The English language version is available at http://www.rijksoverheid.nl/documenten-en-publicaties/brochures/2008/10/20/the-constitution-of-the-kingdom-of-the-netherlands-2008.html [last accessed on 2 June 2014].

Artikel 7
1. Niemand heeft voorafgaand verlof nodig om door de drukpers gedachten of gevoelens te openbaren, behoudens ieders verantwoordelijkheid volgens de wet.
2. De wet stelt regels omtrent radio en televisie. Er is geen voorafgaand toezicht op de inhoud van een radio- of televisieuitzending.
3. Voor het openbaren van gedachten of gevoelens door andere dan in de voorgaande leden genoemde middelen heeft niemand voorafgaand verlof nodig wegens de inhoud daarvan, behoudens ieders verantwoordelijkheid volgens de wet. De wet kan het geven van vertoningen toegankelijk voor personen jonger dan zestien jaar regelen ter bescherming van de goede zeden.
4. De voorgaande leden zijn niet van toepassing op het maken van handelsreclame.

Artikel 8
Het recht tot vereniging wordt erkend. Bij de wet kan dit recht worden beperkt in het belang van de openbare orde.

Artikel 9
1. Het recht tot vergadering en betoging wordt erkend, behoudens ieders verantwoordelijkheid volgens de wet.
2. De wet kan regels stellen ter bescherming van de gezondheid, in het belang van het verkeer en ter bestrijding of voorkoming van wanordelijkheden.
[...]

Artikel 11
Ieder heeft, behoudens bij of krachtens de wet te stellen beperkingen, recht op onaantastbaarheid van zijn lichaam.

1.2 Legal Recognition of Churches and Religious Communities

Dutch law does not define the terms 'church' and 'religious communities'. There is no legal requirement to register such forms of organisation in the Netherlands, neither is there an official register of churches and religious communities. This policy has three basic consequences. First, the lack of a register seemingly contributes to the conditions of the freedom and legal equality of religious communities, as in this manner no formal (institutional or organisational) requirements may be applied with regard to the formal status of religious communities in the Netherlands. In this way, religion and the forms of religious activity (rituals, practices etc.) are neither defined nor 'constructed' by law. Second, religious communities are relatively free to self-define their character, mission and goals. The third consequence, however, is that the state's control over religious communities (and, especially, sects) is very limited.

The legal position of religious communities was set out in the Act on Religious Communities (Wet op de kerkgenootschappen) of 1853,[13] which was replaced in 1988 by the Act on Public Manifestations (Wet openbare manifestaties, hereafter Wom).[14] The Wom regulates the shape of the freedom of religion (the manifestation and expression of religious convictions in particular) and also refers to the very term of 'religious communities' (*kerkgenootschappen*, literally 'church communities') in Art. 3.

Despite the fact that in Dutch law no requirements for registering religious communities have been envisaged, one may indicate certain directions and principles concerning the implicit recognition of churches and other religious communities in the Netherlands. Primarily, one should note the reference to the very term 'religious communities' in Dutch law. One of the examples is the mention of religious organisations in tax law with regard to possible tax exemptions.[15] Moreover, the special status of religious communities has been strengthened by the Civil Code (Burgerlijk Wetboek, hereafter BW), Book 2, Art. 2.2,[16] which has exempted them from a range of legal requirements and regulations. The term 'religious community', despite not being defined *per se*, is separately treated in the system of law and, in a certain sense, represents a form of implicit legal recognition of religious communities. It should also be noted that, since there is no official register, the recognition of an association as a religious community is subject to a decision by the relevant authorities, e.g. a court[17]. This is motivated by a range of privileges and facilities which are assigned to such communities. The use of the term 'kerkgenootschap' in Dutch law has evoked certain doubts and questions regarding the inclusion of all religious communities (e.g. Islamic communities) or just those with legal personality.[18]

13 Wet op de kerkgenootschappen, available at http://www.ntkr.nl/art.php?id=12 [last accessed on 2 June 2014].

14 Wet openbare manifestaties, hereafter Wom, available at http://wetten.overheid.nl/BWBR0004318 [last accessed on 2 June 2014].

15 See Chapter 3.

16 See Subchapter 1.4.

17 Cf. Case 1 below.

18 This is the case e.g. with regard to the reading of the Monumentenwet together with the BW, Book 2. See also Chapter 6.

Jurisprudence

Case 1

In 1986 the Supreme Court (Hoge Raad, hereafter HR) adjudicated on the case of the 'Cloister of St. Walpurga' (*Zusters van Sint Walburga*). The 'Cloister' was a nightclub that operated in Amsterdam, offering sexual services which, in the owners' opinion, were strictly connected with religion, specifically the Dutch Satanic Church. The religious justification (e.g. by emphasising the fertility cult) was an argument the club used for treating it as a religious community. This interpretation would involve the acknowledgement of its autonomy (which could not be impeded through state interference, including the police) and tax exemptions. However, in this case the HR did not find any religious elements and assumed that the club's main activity was offering paid-for sexual services which did not have any religious character in the constitutional sense. The HR did not find any religious elements which would allow for the definition of a religious community and the application of legal instruments aimed at the protection of religious freedom. (HR, 31 October 1986, NJ 1987, 173).

Case 2

Two basic requirements need to be fulfilled in order to define an organisation in terms of a religious community, i.e. 'religion' and 'structure' (HR, 23 July 1942, NJ 1947, 1).[19]

1.3 Registered Religious Communities

The Dutch legislator has not made any regulations regarding the compulsory registering of religious communities or their official recognition. Such communities may operate as associations or other forms of organisation (e.g. foundations). Nevertheless, each organisational form involves specific conditions, facilities and requirements.

1.4 Religious Communities as Associations

In the Netherlands, as in many other European countries, religious communities can adopt the form of private voluntary associations either with or without

19 See also Oldenhuis, Fokko et. al, *Schurende relaties tussen recht en religie* (Assen: Van Gorcum: 2007), p. 84.

legal personality.[20] In cases where such an organisation refers to the principle of the freedom of religion or any other religiously motivated argument, 'the competent administrative or judicial body' is entitled to investigate and adjudicate on the case.[21]

Despite the lack of a legal requirement to register religious communities, the definition of which is not legally stipulated, this very term of religious communities is referred to in Dutch legislation. Moreover, religious communities have a special place in Dutch legislation, and may be classified as 'legal entities *sui generis*'.[22]

The aforementioned legal definition (legal entities *sui generis*) has been applied in Art. 2 of the BW, Book 2, which explicitly refers to religious communities. Religious communities encompassed by the BW have legal personality and are guaranteed a range of legal (and thereby also material) privileges. In this manner, a religious community is exempt from a range of legal requirements and rules that refer to other forms of organisation with legal personality (i.e. organisations which are not defined as religious communities under the terms of the BW). Besides this, the law states that a community's internal statute forms the basis for its activity as long as it does not conflict with Dutch law (Art. 2.2 of the BW, Book 2). In this manner, the separate, special and relatively autonomous character of religious communities has been confirmed. With the exception of Art. 5, other provisions of the BW, Book 2, are not applicable in the case of religious communities.

Islamic communities usually adopt the form of either an association/foundation or a religious community[23] within the meaning laid down in Art. 2.2

20 See e.g. Potz, Richard, Wieshaider, Wolfgang, 'Religious Entities as Legal Persons—Parts of Western and Central Europe (Belgium, Germany, Ireland, Luxemburg, The Netherlands, Austria, The United Kingdom of Great Britain and Northern Ireland)' in *Churches and Other Religious Organisations and Legal Persons*, European Consortium for Church-State Research. Conference, Lars Friedner (ed.) (Leuven: Peeters 2007), p. 28; Doe, Norman, *Law and Religion in Europe. A Comparative Introduction* (New York: Oxford University Press 2011), p. 89.

21 Potz, Wieshaider, 'Religious Entities as Legal Persons ...', p. 28. As the authors further note, this organisational-legal form is often considered beneficial by religious communities, which in this manner, *inter alia*, can maintain relative independence from the state.

22 Rynkowski, Michał, 'Remarks on Art. I-52 of the Constitutional Treaty: New Aspects of the European Ecclesiastical Law?', *German Law Journal*, 11 (2005), p. 1722. See also Oldenhuis, Fokko et. al, *Schurende relaties tussen recht en religie* (Assen: Van Gorcum: 2007), p. 82.

23 In the 1970s, when the issue was broadly debated in the Netherlands, Islamic communities adopted the form of either an association or foundation, which was determined by legal requirements (e.g. the reference to a community's internal statute which at that time was

of the BW, Book 2. One should note however, that although in the context of religious freedom the form adopted by a community does not play a relevant role (as religious freedom is protected separately, regardless of the organisational form), it is significant when it comes to particular organisational and legal matters (e.g. the application of the regulations concerning organisational bodies with legal personality).[24]

Burgerlijk Wetboek Boek 2, Rechtspersonen[25]

Artikel 2
1. Kerkgenootschappen alsmede hun zelfstandige onderdelen en lichamen waarin zij zijn verenigd, bezitten rechtspersoonlijkheid.
2. Zij worden geregeerd door hun eigen statuut, voor zover dit niet in strijd is met de wet. Met uitzondering van artikel 5 gelden de volgende artikelen van deze titel niet voor hen; overeenkomstige toepassing daarvan is geoorloofd, voor zover deze is te verenigen met hun statuut en met de aard der onderlinge verhoudingen.
[...]

Artikel 5
Een rechtspersoon staat wat het vermogensrecht betreft, met een natuurlijk persoon gelijk, tenzij uit de wet het tegendeel voortvloeit.

rather rare for Islamic organisations)—see Landman, Nico, *Kerkgenootschap, stichting of verenlglng: De juridische structuur van islamitische organisaties in Nederland*, pp. 75–76, available at http://www.verenigingrimo.nl/wp/wp-content/uploads/recht8_landman.pdf [last accessed on 11 January 2014]. However, as the author additionally notes, the formal categorisation of a community in terms of a religious community (*kerkgenootschap*) is of secondary significance, as in most cases Islamic organisations are given equal rights and privileges to other religion-based organisations, which are referred to as religious communities. This also proves that in the Dutch case the interpretation of law and legal implementation are of crucial relevance. Nevertheless, the categorisation plays a role with regard to private law—see Oldenhuis et. al, *Schurende relaties ...*, p. 91. Moreover, the status of a religious community protects an organisation against the possibility of legal dissolution based on Art. 2 of the BW, Book 2.

24 See Oldenhuis, Fokko et. al, *Schurende relaties tussen recht en religie*, (Assen: Van Gorcum: 2007), p. 91.

25 Burgerlijk Wetboek Boek 2, Rechtspersonen, available at www.wetten.overheid.nl/BWBR0003045/ [last accessed on 2 June 2014].

Jurisprudence

Case 1

Islamic associations or foundations are not treated as religious communities in terms of Art. 2 of the BW, Book 2. In its adjudication the court referred to the accepted definition of such a community in the sense of Art. 2, BW, Book 2, i.e. a religious community with an organised structure. Islamic organisations can also choose the form of a religious community defined in the BW. In the case of other forms of organisation, both the provisions of Dutch civil law and an organisation's inner statute form the legal foundation for their activity. Moreover, neither the legislator nor the courts are competent to adjudicate on the religious (e.g. Islamic) profile of an organisation or the conformity of an organisation's operation with specific religious rules and traditions. (e.g. Rechtbank 's-Hertogenbosch 29 December 2006, ECLI:NL:RBSHE:2006:AZ5352)[26]

---

26 Available at http://uitspraken.rechtspraak.nl/inziendocument?id=ECLI:NL:RBSHE:2006:AZ5352 [last accessed on 10 February 2014].

CHAPTER 2

Relations between the State and Islam

2.1 Introduction

After World War II, as a consequence both of the decolonisation process and the flow of labour immigrants, Dutch society was becoming increasingly pluralised. This process was considerably influenced by the increasing presence of Muslims from the 1960s, initially primarily from Turkey, Morocco, and Suriname.[1]

The first political concepts of integrating Islamic minorities entailed the adaptation of elements of Islamic culture on Dutch socio-political grounds. At the same time, the organisations representing Islamic minorities, which were established at that time, concentrated on internal integration based on shared religious values and common elements of ethnic identity. The unification of religious, ideological and ethnic issues within Islamic interest groups had further implications. Muslims began to form their political postulations, which were aimed at maintaining their self-identity and self-awareness. These demands were becoming increasingly audible and concerned issues such as e.g. the legal conditions of imams' presence, the recognition of Islamic feasts and traditions (such as circumcision and ritual slaughtering) and the opportunity to establish their own separate prayer houses.[2]

In the 1980s the main demands of Islamic communities concerned religious practices, primarily in their organisational dimension.[3] The number of Muslims was systematically increasing from the 1970s onwards, mainly due to the policy of family reunion. At the same time one may observe the Dutch government's growing interest in the presence and activism of Muslims. The beginning of the public debate on the role and position of Islam in the Dutch public

1 Koning, Martijn de, 'Netherlands' in *Yearbook of Muslims in Europe*, Vol. 1, Jorgen S. Nielsen et. al. (eds.) (Leiden: Brill, 2009), p. 243; Bernts, Tom, Jong, Gert de, Yar, Hasan, 'Een religieuze atlas van Nederland' in *Geloven in het publieke domein. Verkenningen van een dubbele transformatie*, Wim B.H.J. van de Donk et al. (Amsterdam: Amsterdam University Press, 2006), p. 113.

2 Zdanowski, Jerzy, 'Muzułmanie w Holandii', in *Muzułmanie w Europie*, Anna Parzymies (ed.) (Warszawa: Wyd. Akademickie DIALOG, 2005), pp. 423–425.

3 Sunier, Thijl, 'Moslims in de Nederlandse politieke arena', in *Emancipatie en subcultuur. Sociale bewegingen in België en Nederland*, Thijl Sunier et. al. (eds.) (Amsterdam: Instituut voor Publiek en Politiek, 2000), p. 152.

sphere dates back to the 1990s. According to Jerzy Zdanowski, this political and social discussion concentrated on 'freedom of religion, equality under the law and the separation of church and state'[4]—principles which touched both the social and legal order.

Dutch Muslims, amongst whom Turks (38 per cent) and Moroccans (31 per cent) have formed the majority, represent approximately 5 per cent of the Dutch population.[5] Interestingly enough, sociological research has indicated an increase in the popularity of Islamic culture among groups with those ethnic backgrounds. Thus one may conclude that religion is a factor of group integration.[6]

Muslims have never formed any single monolithic Islamic community. Instead, they have been organised within a number of subgroups and communities representing various Islamic streams and traditions.[7] For a long time, this factor formed a relevant obstacle in attempts to establish one Islamic body that would officially represent the interests of Islamic communities in their relations with the government. Despite the endeavours made in the 1970s, Muslims did not elect any representative bodies. Subsequent attempts to combine their influence into one group also failed to have a positive effect. In turn, the lack of a representative body hindered their formal relationship with the Dutch Government. It was not until the beginning of the 21st century that Muslims created such institutions. Currently, the representative body of Dutch Muslims is the CMO,[8] which plays an advisory role in relations with the Dutch government,

4 See Zdanowski, 'Muzułmanie w Holandii', pp. 423–425.

5 Among non-western Muslims in the Netherlands one can also distinguish minorities from Suriname, Afghanistan, Iraq, Somalia, Pakistan, Iran, Egypt, Indonesia and Tunisia. Herten, Marieke van, Otten, Ferdy, *Naar een nieuwe schatting van het aantal islamieten in Nederland*, Centraal Bureau voor de Statistiek, Bevolkingstrends 2007, available at http://www.cbs.nl/NR/rdonlyres/ACE89EBE-0785-4664-9973-A6A00A457A55/0/2007k3b15p48art.pdf [last accessed on 1 March 2014]; *Ruim 850 duizend islamieten in Nederland*, 24 October 2007, available at http://www.cbs.nl/nl-NL/menu/themas/bevolking/publicaties/artikelen/archief/2007/2007-2278-wm.htm [last accessed on 1 March 2014].

6 Hooven, Marcel ten, 'Religie verdeelt Nederland', in *Ongewenste goden. De publieke rol van religie in Nederland*, Marcel ten Hooven, Theo de Wit (eds) (Amsterdam: Uitgeverij SUN, 2006), p. 18.

7 See Bernts, Jong de, Yar, 'Een religieuze atlas ...', pp. 114–126.

8 In 2005 the Dutch Contact Group Islam (*Contactgroep Islam*, hereafter CGI) was recognised as the second body representing Islamic communities in their relations with the government. The CGI united a considerably smaller number of organisations than the CMO, i.e. the Union of Lahore Ahmadiyya Muslim Organisations in the Netherlands (Unie van Lahore Ahmadiyya Moslim Organisatie Nederland, ULAMON), the Federation of Alevi-Bektashi associations

e.g. via regular participation in meetings with the Dutch Minister of Integration and Immigration.[9]

2.2 The Contact Body of Muslims and the Government (CMO)

In 2004 the Dutch state recognised the Contact Body of Muslims and the Government (*Contactorgaan Moslims en Overheid*, hereafter CMO) as the representative of twelve Islamic umbrella organisations[10] incorporating the vast majority of Muslims in the Netherlands.[11] The role of the CMO has not been limited to the formal advocacy of shared interests. The CMO also has the right to initiate certain organisational and structural solutions, as well as to express its opinions on candidates for the positions of religious ministers (chaplains) before official ministerial nominations.[12] Neither the position nor the organisation of the CMO has been legally defined.

(Federatie van Alevitische en Bektashistische verenigingen, HAK.DER), Sjiite Council (Sjiietische Raad). See Vellenga, Sipco et al., *Mist in de polder. Zicht op ontwikkelingen omtrent de islam in Nederland* (Amsterdam: Aksant, 2009), p. 74. Currently the CGI does not play an active advisory role. Moreover, aside from the CMO and the CGI, a number of other Islamic organisations in the Netherlands can be defined. See Koning de, 'Netherlands', pp. 247–248.

9 Koning de, 'Netherlands', p. 247.

10 I.e. Islamic Foundation Netherlands (Islamitische Stichting Nederland, ISN), Union of Moroccan Mosque Organisations The Netherlands (Unie van Marokkaanse Moskee Organisaties in Nederland, UMMON), Dutch Islamic Federation (Nederlandse Islamitische Federatie, NIF), Milli Görüs The Netherlands (Milli Görüs Nederland, MGN), Foundation Islamic Centre the Netherlands (Stichting Islamitisch Centrum Nederland, SICN), World Islamic Mission (WIM), Sjiite Association (Overkoepelende Shiïetische Vereniging, OSV), Islamic Association of Bosnians in the Netherlands (Islamitische Vereniging voor Bosniaks in Nederland, IVBN), Turkish Islamic Cultural Foundation (Turks Islamitische Culturele Federatie, TICF), Dutch Islamic Council (Nederlandse Islamitische Raad, NIR), National Platform of New Muslims (Landelijk Platform Nieuwe Moslims, LPNM), Turkish Federation the Netherlands (Turkse Federatie Nederland, TFN). http://cmoweb.nl/index.php/component/content/article?id=74 [last accessed on 11 January 2014]; [translation of the organisations' names—following Koning de, 'Netherlands', pp. 246–247, and own translation]

11 According to the CMO, it incorporates 84% of all mosques in the Netherlands. http://cmoweb.nl/index.php/component/content/article?id=73 [last accessed on 11 January 2014].

12 See Chapter 10.

CHAPTER 3

State Support for Islamic Religious Communities

The Dutch state does not directly support any activities which are of a solely religious character. This principle is based on the interpretation of the separation of church and state, and state neutrality. Before 1983, the Dutch state had financially supported (Protestant) churches, by e.g. covering clergy salaries.[1] In the second half of the 19th century, the first proposals of constitutional reforms had already appeared with regard to the rules of the state funding of churches. The relevant political developments accelerated in the mid 20th century when the three following advisory commissions were established: the Van Walsum Commission (*Commissie-Van Walsum*, 1946), the Van Schaik State Commission (*Staatscommissie-Van Schaik*, 1954)[2] and the Verdam Commission (*Commissie-Verdam*, 1970). Eventually, on 7 December 1983, the Act Abolishing Financial Relations between the State and Church (Wet beëindiging financiële verhouding tussen staat en kerk)[3] was introduced. On 10 July 1995 the constitutional article allowing state salaries for the clergy was abolished, thereby dissolving *direct* financial relations between the Dutch state and churches.

Current Dutch law excludes any forms of privileging religious communities and/or their activities. Nevertheless, certain forms of indirect (financial) support are possible on general grounds (e.g. state support for the renovation of monuments, subsidies for schools and other institutions).[4] Socio-cultural (but

1 Bijsterveld, Sophie C. van, *Państwo i kościół w Holandii* in *Państwo i kościół w krajach Unii Europejskiej*, G. Robbers (ed.) (Wrocław: Kolonia Limited 2007), p. 181; The Report of the Walsum Commission: *De financiële betrekkingen tussen de staat en de kerken. Rapport van de Staatscommissie voor de Zaken van de Erediensten*, Zitting 1968–1969, 10030, no. 2, pp. 5–6, available at http://resourcessgd.kb.nl/SGD/19681969/PDF/SGD_19681969_0003474.pdf [last accessed on 2 June 2014],

2 Bijsterveld van, *Godsdienstvrijheid ...*, pp. 78–80.

3 Wet beëindiging financiële verhouding tussen staat en kerk, available at http://wetten.overheid.nl/BWBR0003640 [last accessed on 7 February 2014]. The Act was preceded by a broad consultation with the representatives of religious communities in the Netherlands. Muslim representatives were not involved (the Act encompasses the regulations concerning religious communities which were traditionally present in the Netherlands at the time).

4 See e.g. Potz, Wieshaider, 'Religious Entities as Legal Persons ...', p. 35.

not religious *per se*) activities which are organised or performed by religious communities can be subsidised by the State Treasury on the same grounds as for any other organisations. However, organisations which perform activities of a strictly religious character (and in this manner do not act in the interests of the 'general public' but represent narrow worldview interests) are in principle refused subsidies for such activities. This is justified by the notions of state neutrality and the separation of church and state. At the same time, an organisation cannot be disqualified solely due to its religious profile if it is possible to subsidise its activity on general grounds. In such a case, the refusal would infringe the constitutional principle of the freedom of religion. Providing all the formal (general) requirements are met, the subsidy cannot be refused.

As previously indicated, Dutch law does not ban contacts between state (including local) authorities and religious communities. Such relations may take place at both national and local levels—at the local level municipal councils (*gemeenteraden*) are competent to decide in this regard.[5] Moreover, regarding state support of religious (including Islamic) communities, direct and indirect as well as material and non-material forms should be distinguished. In this manner, Islamic cultural activities,[6] the maintenance of mosques and prayer houses,[7] as well as the presence of chaplains in public institutions,[8] may be supported by the state.

Jurisprudence

Case 1

A religious community can be refused subsidies for social work by municipal authorities if the general conditions of such subsidies are not in accordance with the municipality's policy. The policy of subsidising religiously-oriented organisations should be based on the principle of their (mutual) equality, i.e. a

---

5 Regarding the general rules of such arrangements at a local level, and the bounds of a municipality's flexibility in this regard, see the ministerial guidelines included in *Tweeluik religie en publiek domein. Handvatten voor gemeenten*, Vereniging van Nederlandse Gemeenten, Ministerie van Binnenlandse Zaken en Koninkrijksrelaties, maart 2009, pp. 14–16, available at http://www.vng.nl/files/vng/vng/Documenten/Extranet/Gemeenterecht/2009/Tweeluik%20Religie%20en%20publiek%20domein.pdf [last accessed on 20 January 2014].

6 The framework of such subsidies is created at the level of provinces, where the general conditions are usually shaped.

7 See Chapter 6.

8 See Chapter 10.

particular religious conviction may be neither excluded nor privileged.[9] (ABRS, 19 December 1996, AB 1997, 414).

3.1 Tax Exemptions

Since the 1960s[10] the Dutch tax system has allowed tax deductions for public benefit organisations (including e.g. cultural and religious organisations and institutions). This principle has been maintained in the Act on Income Tax (Wet Inkomstenbelasting 2001, hereafter Wet IB 2001).[11] The regulations concerning such contributions are set out in the Regulation of the Minister of Finance, i.e. Income Tax, Contributions and Public Benefit Organisations (Inkomstenbelasting, giften en algemeen nut beogende instellingen) of 6 April 2010. In the regulation the rules for *direct* donations for religious communities are defined (Art. 4).[12] The detailed conditions concerning contributions and tax facilities for religious communites, defined in terms of public benefit organisations (*algemene nut instellingen*), are further defined in the respective implementing regulation (Uitvoeringsregeling Algemene wet inzake rijksbelastingen) of the Minister of Finance.

---

9 See Bok, A.J., *Subsidies*, Mon. Awb A6, (Gouda: Kluwer 2002), pp. 108–109; Davelaar, Maarten, Smits van Waesberghe, Eliane, *Tussen principes en pragmatisme. Een onderzoek onder Nederlandse gemeenten naar de subsidiëring van levensbeschouwelijke organisaties* (Utrecht: FORUM, Instituut voor Multiculturele Vraagstukken, 2010), p. 18, available online at http://www.forum.nl/Portals/0/publicaties/Tussen-principes-en-pragmatisme.pdf [last accessed on 22 January 2014].

10 The respective acts from 1964 and 1969. See Bijsterveld van, *Godsdienstvrijheid* ..., pp. 85–86.

11 It is worth noting that since 1 January 2014, new regulations have been introduced on the basis of the Wijziging van de Uitvoeringsregeling Algemene wet inzake rijksbelastingen 1994 of 12 July 2013, No. DB 2013/366 M, available at https://zoek.officielebekendmakingen.nl/stcrt-2013-20451.html [last accessed on 4 January 2014]. With regard to religious communities see Uitvoeringsregeling Algemene wet inzake rijksbelastingen 1994, Art. 1a: 7f and h (requirements concerning the information about a community and the transparency of financial reports), available at http://wetten.overheid.nl/BWBR0006736 [last accessed on 4 January 2014].

12 See also Chapter 6.

Wet inkomstenbelasting 2001[13]

Artikel 6.32. Aftrekbare giften
1. Aftrekbare giften zijn:
a. periodieke giften;
b. andere giften.
[...]

Artikel 6.33. Definities
In deze afdeling en de daarop berustende bepalingen wordt verstaan onder:
a. giften: bevoordelingen uit vrijgevigheid en verplichte bijdragen waar geen directe tegenprestatie tegenover staat;
b. instellingen: algemeen nut beogende instellingen;
c. verenigingen: niet aan de vennootschapsbelasting onderworpen of daarvan vrijgestelde verenigingen met volledige rechtsbevoegdheid en met ten minste 25 leden, gevestigd in een lidstaat van de Europese Unie, Aruba, Curaçao, Sint Maarten, een bij ministeriële regeling aangewezen mogendheid of op de BES eilanden.

Artikel 6.34. Periodieke giften
Periodieke giften zijn giften in de vorm van vaste en gelijkmatige periodieke uitkeringen die eindigen uiterlijk bij overlijden, aan instellingen of verenigingen.

Artikel 6.35. Andere giften
Andere giften zijn giften aan instellingen of aan steunstichtingen SBBI.
[...]

Artikel 6.38. Het in aanmerking nemen van periodieke giften
1. Periodieke giften worden in aanmerking genomen indien zij berusten op een bij notariële of onderhandse akte van schenking aangegane verplichting om de uitkeringen of verstrekkingen gedurende vijf of meer jaren ten minste jaarlijks uit te keren.
2. Bij ministeriële regeling worden regels gesteld waaraan de onderhandse akte van schenking, bedoeld in het eerste lid, moet voldoen.

13 Wet inkomstenbelasting 2001, available at http://wetten.overheid.nl/BWBR0011353 [last accessed on 3 June 2014].

Artikel 6.39. Omvang in aanmerking te nemen andere giften
1. Andere giften worden in aanmerking genomen voorzover zij met schriftelijke bescheiden kunnen worden gestaafd en voorzover zij samen zowel € 60 als 1% van het verzamelinkomen vóór toepassing van de persoonsgebonden aftrek te boven gaan, en vervolgens tot ten hoogste 10% van het verzamelinkomen vóór toepassing van de persoonsgebonden aftrek.
[...]

Inkomstenbelasting, giften en algemeen nut beogende instellingen[14]

4. Giften aan kerkelijke instellingen
Bedragen die rechtstreeks aan geestelijken ter beschikking worden gesteld voor doeleinden die de kerkelijke instelling nastreeft of voor het verrichten van religieuze handelingen, worden aangemerkt als giften aan de kerkelijke instelling. Bijdragen voor kerkelijk wijkwerk, stipendia, voor het lezen van missen, huwelijksinzegening, doop en dergelijke bijzondere kerkelijke plechtigheden zijn giften als de bijdragen ten bate van de kerkelijke instelling of van de geestelijke als zodanig komen. In deze gevallen moet de betaling van de bedoelde bedragen blijken uit schriftelijke bewijsstukken.

Uitvoeringsregeling Algemene wet inzake rijksbelastingen 1994[15]

Artikel 1a
1. Een instelling wordt door de inspecteur aangemerkt als een algemeen nut beogende instelling indien en zolang:
a. uit de regelgeving en de feitelijke werkzaamheden van de instelling blijkt dat de instelling met het totaal van haar algemeen nuttige activiteiten geen winstoogmerk heeft;
b. uit de regelgeving en de feitelijke werkzaamheden van de instelling blijkt dat de instelling uitsluitend of nagenoeg uitsluitend het algemeen belang dient;
c. uit de regelgeving van de instelling en de feiten blijkt dat een natuurlijk persoon noch een rechtspersoon over het vermogen van de instelling kan beschikken als ware het zijn eigen vermogen, met dien verstande dat de

14 Inkomstenbelasting, giften en algemeen nut beogende instellingen, available at http://wetten.overheid.nl/BWBR0027503 [last accessed on 3 June 2014].

15 Uitvoeringsregeling Algemene wet inzake rijksbelastingen 1994, available at http://wetten.overheid.nl/BWBR0006736 [last accessed on 4 January 2014]

inspecteur, zo nodig onder door hem te stellen voorwaarden, kan toestaan dat een steunstichting en de instelling of instellingen welke door deze stichting wordt ondersteund, onderscheidenlijk worden ondersteund, over en weer kunnen beschikken over elkaars vermogen als ware het eigen vermogen;
d. de instelling niet meer vermogen aanhoudt dan is aangegeven in artikel 1b;
e. de leden van het orgaan van de instelling dat het beleid bepaalt, ter zake van de door hen in die hoedanigheid voor de instelling verrichte werkzaamheden geen andere beloning ontvangen dan een vergoeding voor gemaakte onkosten en een niet-bovenmatig vacatiegeld;
f. de instelling beschikt over een actueel beleidsplan dat inzicht geeft in de door de instelling te verrichten werkzaamheden ter verwezenlijking van haar doelstelling, de wijze van werving van inkomsten, het beheer van het vermogen van de instelling en de besteding daarvan;
g. de beheerkosten van de instelling in redelijke verhouding staan tot de bestedingen ten behoeve van het doel van de instelling;
h. uit de regelgeving van de instelling blijkt dat bij opheffing van de instelling een batig liquidatiesaldo wordt besteed ten behoeve van een algemeen nut beogende instelling met een soortgelijke doelstelling of van een buitenlandse instelling die uitsluitend of nagenoeg uitsluitend het algemeen nut beoogt en die een soortgelijke doelstelling heeft;
i. de administratie van de instelling zodanig is ingericht dat daaruit duidelijk blijkt:
1°. de aard en omvang van de aan de afzonderlijke leden van het orgaan van de instelling dat het beleid bepaalt toekomende onkostenvergoedingen en vacatiegelden;
2°. de aard en omvang van de kosten die door de instelling zijn gemaakt ten behoeve van het beheer van de instelling, alsmede de aard en omvang van de andere uitgaven van de instelling;
3°. de aard en omvang van de inkomsten van de instelling, en
4°. de aard en omvang van het vermogen van de instelling, en
j. de instelling via internet op elektronische wijze informatie met betrekking tot haar functioneren, openbaar maakt.
2. Een algemeen nut beogende instelling mag ter financiering van haar doelstelling commerciële activiteiten ontplooien, indien de inkomsten, zijnde het saldo van baten en lasten, gerealiseerd met die activiteiten, in overeenstemming met artikel 1b, binnen een redelijke termijn geheel of nagenoeg geheel ten goede komen aan die doelstelling.
3. De beschikking waarbij een instelling wordt aangemerkt als een algemeen nut beogende instelling kan terugwerken tot en met een voor dagtekening daarvan gelegen datum.

4. De inspecteur maakt het aanmerken van een instelling als een algemeen nut beogende instelling op een daartoe geschikte wijze publiek bekend. Het niet meer als zodanig aanmerken wordt ook op een daartoe geschikte wijze publiek bekendgemaakt.
5. Onder algemeen nuttige activiteiten worden voor de toepassing van dit artikel verstaan: alle activiteiten die erop zijn gericht om de doelstelling van een algemeen nut beogende instelling te verwezenlijken of te bevorderen. Activiteiten zijn geen algemeen nuttige activiteiten indien de instelling het geheel van die activiteiten tegen commerciële tarieven verricht.
6. Onder commerciële activiteiten worden voor de toepassing van dit artikel verstaan: het tegen commerciële tarieven verrichten van werkzaamheden of verlenen van diensten met het oogmerk hiermee ter financiering van de algemeen nuttige activiteiten van de instelling een positief resultaat te behalen.
7. De informatie, bedoeld in het eerste lid, onderdeel j, bestaat ten minste uit:
a. de naam van de instelling;
b. het nummer, bedoeld in artikel 12, onderdeel a, van de Handelsregisterwet 2007, van de instelling, dan wel ingeval de instelling is gevestigd in een staat als bedoeld in artikel 1c, het voor deze regeling door de Nederlandse Belastingdienst verstrekte fiscaal nummer;
c. het post- of bezoekadres, dan wel het telefoonnummer, dan wel het e-mailadres van de instelling;
d. de doelstelling volgens de regelgeving van de instelling;
e. de hoofdlijnen van het actuele beleidsplan, bedoeld in het eerste lid, onderdeel f, van de instelling;
f. de bestuurssamenstelling, het beloningsbeleid van de instelling en de namen van de bestuurders, met uitzondering van:
1° de namen van bestuurders van kerkgenootschappen alsmede hun zelfstandige onderdelen en lichamen waarin zij zijn verenigd, en
2° de namen van bestuurders waarvoor de inspecteur op verzoek van de instelling ontheffing verleent omdat is aangetoond dat publicatie van deze namen een reëel gevaar oplevert voor de persoonlijke veiligheid van deze bestuurders of van hun familieleden;
g. een actueel verslag van de uitgeoefende activiteit of activiteiten van de instelling;
h. de balans en de staat van baten en lasten, met toelichting, van de instelling dan wel, indien het instellingen betreft die niet actief geld of goederen werven onder derden en die het aan hen ter beschikking staande vermogen of de opbrengsten daarvan uitsluitend of nagenoeg uitsluitend besteden ten behoeve van hun doelstelling (zuivere vermogensfondsen) of indien het kerkgenootschappen alsmede hun zelfstandige onderdelen en lichamen waarin

zij zijn verenigd betreft, de staat van baten en lasten en een overzicht van de voorgenomen bestedingen, met toelichting.
8. De informatie, bedoeld in het zevende lid, onderdeel h, wordt telkens binnen zes maanden na afloop van het boekjaar openbaar gemaakt.

Artikel 1b
1. Een algemeen nut beogende instelling houdt niet meer vermogen aan dan redelijkerwijs nodig is voor de continuïteit van de voorziene werkzaamheden ten behoeve van de doelstelling van de instelling.
2. Onder vermogen dat nodig is voor de continuïteit van de voorziene werkzaamheden als bedoeld in het eerste lid worden begrepen:
a. vermogen of bestanddelen daarvan die krachtens uiterste wilsbeschikking of schenking door de instelling zijn verkregen, en die op grond van aan die uiterste wilsbeschikking of schenking verbonden voorwaarden, al dan niet in reële termen, in stand moeten worden gehouden;
b. vermogensbestanddelen voor zover de instandhouding daarvan voortvloeit uit de doelstelling van die instelling, en
c. activa en voor de voorziene aanschaf van activa aangehouden vermogensbestanddelen, voor zover een instelling die activa redelijkerwijs nodig heeft ten behoeve van de doelstelling van de instelling.
3. De algemeen nut beogende instelling vermeldt in haar financiële administratie het doel waarvoor het vermogen wordt aangehouden, alsmede een motivering voor de omvang van dat vermogen.

Jurisprudence

Case 1

A contribution to a mosque trust was submitted by a Muslim. The contribution was declared as a tax deduction for a public benefit organisation. The respondent was not able to submit the mosque's annual financial report, nor any bank records as the contribution was made in cash, in accordance with Islamic tradition. The Court however held that the contribution conformed to the tax law and should be recognised for tax deduction purposes. (Rechtbank Haarlem, 11 October 2006, ECLI:NL:RBHAA:2006:AZ0603)[16]

16 Available at http://uitspraken.rechtspraak.nl/inziendocument?id=ECLI:NL:RBHAA:2006:AZ0603 [last accessed on 2 June 2014].

CHAPTER 4

Muslims in Integration Law

The increasingly pluralised nature of Dutch society has considerably influenced the direction of the government's activity regarding integration policy. Here, religious differences can be distinguished as one of the crucial issues in current public debate in the Netherlands, e.g. ritual slaughter, the headscarf issue, blasphemy and the inclusion of Islamic traditions and holidays in the Dutch system of law. The presence and activity of Islamic communities in the Netherlands have contributed to the development of political and legislative discussion on the shape of Dutch society and culture.[1] In terms of integration, one should note the special relevance of the system of education, Dutch language and work opportunities.[2] The role of these factors was emphasised in the Act on the Naturalisation of Newcomers (Wet inburgering nieuwkomers, hereafter the WIN) of 1998,[3] which was replaced in 2007 by the Act on Naturalisation (Wet inburgering, hereafter WI). The Dutch integration policy is based on the idea of non-discrimination.[4]

1 See also the Memorandum of the Ministry of Immigration and Integration concerning integration issues (Nota Weerbaarheid en integratiebeleid. Preventie van radicalisering vanuit het perspectief van het integratiebeleid, Tweede Kamer 2004–2005, 29754, no. 27), available at https://zoek.officielebekendmakingen.nl/kst-29754-27.html [last accessed on 20 January 2014]. The document was discussed with the representatives of the CMO and CGI. With regard to integration policy, one should also refer e.g. to the WPO (Art. 8 § 3) which is, according to the law, aimed at deepening social integration—see also Subchapter 8.1. As stipulated in Art. 9 § 10, the language of the education provided is Dutch.

2 See Nota *Integratie in het perspectief van immigratie*, Tweede Kamer 2001–2002, 28198, no. 2, available at https://zoek.officielebekendmakingen.nl/dossier/28198/kst-28198-2?resultIndex=3&sorttype=1&sortorder=4 [last accessed on 24 January 2014], where the state's support of the organisation of imam training in the Netherlands was also indicated.

3 See Art. 4.2 of the Wet inburgering nieuwkomers, available at http://wetten.overheid.nl/BWBR0009544/geldigheidsdatum_31-12-2006 [last accessed on 3 January 2014]. In this regard, see also a crucial document on the development of Dutch policy toward minorities, i.e. *Minderhedenbeleid*, Tweede Kamer 1982–1983, 16102, no. 20–21, available at http://resourcessgd.kb.nl/SGD/19821983/PDF/SGD_19821983_0002222.pdf [last accessed on 19 January 2014]. In this document (pp. 110–112), the special role of religion in the integration process was emphasised, as well as the necessity to introduce legal regulations aiming to facilitate the fulfillment of religious freedom, e.g. with reference to ritual slughter issues and burial traditions, the presence of religious ministers and the shape of education.

4 Here, one should also refer to the Royal Act on Dutch Nationality (Rijkswet op het Ne-

In the Dutch process of policy-making, Islamic organisations (the CMO and CGI) have been involved with regard to issues which touch Islamic traditions, practices and activities, and their representatives have participated in meetings with the government. The Dutch system of law does not explicitly refer to Islamic communities with regard to integration policy,[5] but it does refer e.g. to the requirements concerning the presence of chaplains or religious ministers.

In the mid-1990s the Ministry for Internal Affairs proposed obligatory education for imams. Moreover, according to this proposal, imams were obliged to submit naturalisation documents (*inburgeringscontract*). It was proposed that decisions on granting Islamic clergy the right to stay in the Netherlands should be taken on the basis of their knowledge of the Dutch language and culture. This has, however, evoked some objections in that these initiatives would allow the state to control and interfere in religious communities' internal affairs.[6]

The WI includes the obligatory naturalisation of chaplains (Art. 3.1),[7] which has been maintained in order to increase imams' links with Dutch culture and society, and thereby also to strengthen the process of integration.[8] In this manner the role of imams has been considered to exceed the religious dimension, which may be illustrated by the notion of the polder-imam (*polderimam*) which was coined in the course of the debate.[9]

---

derlanderschap) of 19 December 1984, as amended, available at http://wetten.overheid.nl/BWBR0003738 [last accessed on 1 March 2014].

5 Here, ethnic and not merely religious issues have been referred to in the Dutch system of law.

6 Shadid, Wasif A.R., Koningsveld, Peter S. van, *Islam in Nederland en België. Religieuze institutionalisering in twee landen met een gemeenschappelijke voorgeschiedenis*, (Leuven: Peeters, 2008), pp. 67–69.

7 The law concerns newcomers from non-EU countries.

8 *Imams in Nederland? Wie leidt ze op? Rapport van de Adviescommissie Imamopleidingen*, December 2003, p. 7, available at http://www.rijksoverheid.nl/documenten-en-publicaties/rapporten/2005/10/14/imams-in-nederland-wie-leidt-ze-op.html [last accessed on 18 January 2014].

9 The term 'polder-imam' is used with reference to imams who can function as imams due to their knowledge of Islam and respect from their community, and, at the same time, have already been properly 'rooted' in Dutch culture and know how Dutch society functions, and what principles and values form the cultural foundation of the Netherlands. See Douwes, Dick, Koning, Martijn de, Boender, Welmoet, *Nederlandse moslims: van migrant tot burger* (Amsterdam: Amsterdam University Press—Salomé 2005), pp. 89–90.

The conditions of a chaplain's permission to stay have also been included in the Regulation on Aliens 2000 (Vreemdelingenbesluit 2000), in Art. 3.33 and Art. 3.71. Moreover, the provisions of the Act on Foreigners (Vreemdelingenwet, hereafter Vw) refer to the implementation of Directive 2003/109/EC concerning the status of third-country nationals who are long-term residents. The Vw also includes the regulations concerning asylum conditions, based on a well-founded fear of persecution in a refugee's country.

As one of the significant elements in Dutch integration policy one may recognise the solutions in the field of election law. As laid down in Art. B3 of the Voting Act (Kieswet), non-citizens residing in the Netherlands have the right to vote (and to be elected) in local elections if they have resided legally in the country for at least five years.

Wet inburgering of 30 November 2006[10]

Hoofdstuk 1. Inleidende bepalingen

Artikel 1
1. In deze wet en de daarop berustende bepalingen wordt verstaan onder:
a. Onze Minister: Onze Minister van Sociale Zaken en Werkgelegenheid;
b. inburgeringsplichtige: de persoon die op grond van de artikelen 3, 5 en 6 inburgeringsplichtig is;
c. leerplichtige leeftijd: de leeftijd waarop bij verblijf in Nederland sprake is van een verplichting tot inschrijving als bedoeld in artikel 3 van de Leerplichtwet 1969;
d. inburgeringsplicht: de verplichting, bedoeld in artikel 7;
e. geestelijke bedienaar: de persoon die een geestelijk, godsdienstig of levensbeschouwelijk ambt bekleedt, arbeid verricht als geestelijk voorganger, godsdienstleraar of zendeling, dan wel ten behoeve van een kerkgenootschap of een ander genootschap op geestelijke of levensbeschouwelijke grondslag werkzaamheden van overwegend godsdienstige, geestelijke of levensbeschouwelijke aard verricht;
f. inburgeringsexamen: het examen, bedoeld in artikel 7, tweede lid, onderdeel a;

10 Wet inburgering, available at http://wetten.overheid.nl/BWBR0020611 [last accessed on 9 January 2014]. One of the relevant amendments to the law entails the requirement of self-funding. On 31 January 2013 the government ceased to cover the costs of naturalisation. See http://www.rijksoverheid.nl/onderwerpen/inburgering-en-integratie/inburgering-en-integratie-in-nederland [last accessed on 11 January 2014].

g. burgerservicenummer: het als zodanig overeenkomstig de Wet algemene bepalingen burgerservicenummer aan een natuurlijke persoon toegekend nummer;
h. kwalificatieplicht: de plicht tot inschrijving als bedoeld in artikel 4a, eerste lid, van de Leerplichtwet 1969.
2. Bij regeling van Onze Minister kan de geestelijke bedienaar, bedoeld in het eerste lid, onderdeel e, nader worden omschreven.

Artikel 2
Een minderjarige is bekwaam de rechtshandelingen te verrichten die noodzakelijk zijn met betrekking tot de uitoefening, onderscheidenlijk de nakoming van de voor hem uit deze wet en de daarop berustende bepalingen voortvloeiende rechten en verplichtingen.

Hoofdstuk 2. Inburgeringsplicht

Artikel 3
1. Inburgeringsplichtig is de vreemdeling, die rechtmatig verblijf verkrijgt in de zin van artikel 8, onderdelen a en c, van de Vreemdelingenwet 2000, die:
a. anders dan voor een tijdelijk doel in Nederland verblijft, of
b. geestelijke bedienaar is.
2. Bij algemene maatregel van bestuur worden regels gesteld over het voortduren van de inburgeringsplicht in geval van tijdelijke beëindiging van de in het eerste lid bedoelde omstandigheden.
3. Bij of krachtens algemene maatregel van bestuur worden regels gesteld omtrent het tijdelijke doel, bedoeld in het eerste lid, waarbij zo veel mogelijk wordt aangesloten bij het verblijfsrecht van tijdelijke aard, bedoeld in artikel 21, eerste lid, onderdeel b, van de Vreemdelingenwet 2000.
4. De inburgeringsplicht, bedoeld in het eerste lid, wordt niet met terugwerkende kracht gevestigd.
[...]

Artikel 5
1. In afwijking van artikel 3 is niet inburgeringsplichtig degene die:
a. jonger dan 16 jaar is dan wel de pensioengerechtigde leeftijd, bedoeld in artikel 7a, eerste lid, van de Algemene Ouderdomswet, heeft bereikt;
b. ten minste acht jaren tijdens de leerplichtige leeftijd in Nederland heeft verbleven;
c. beschikt over een bij of krachtens algemene maatregel van bestuur aangewezen diploma, certificaat of ander document;

d. leerplichtig of kwalificatieplichtig is;
e. aansluitend op de leerplicht of kwalificatieplicht een opleiding volgt waarvan de afronding leidt tot uitreiking van een krachtens onderdeel c aangewezen diploma, certificaat of ander document.
2. Evenmin is inburgeringsplichtig:
a. de persoon die onderdaan is van een lidstaat van de Europese Unie, een andere staat die partij is bij de Overeenkomst betreffende de Europese Economische Ruimte, of Zwitserland;
b. het familielid van de persoon, bedoeld in onderdeel a, dat onderdaan is van een derde staat en dat uit hoofde van richtlijn 2004/38/EG, de Overeenkomst betreffende de Europese Economische Ruimte dan wel de Overeenkomst tussen de Europese Gemeenschappen en haar lidstaten, enerzijds, en de Zwitserse Bondsstaat, anderzijds, over het vrije verkeer van personen, gerechtigd is Nederland binnen te komen en er te verblijven;
c. de vreemdeling die ingevolge de wetgeving van een lidstaat van de Europese Unie of een andere staat die partij is bij de Overeenkomst betreffende de Europese Economische Ruimte heeft voldaan aan een inburgeringsvereiste om de status van langdurig ingezetene in de zin van richtlijn 2003/109/EG van 25 november 2003 betreffende de status van langdurig ingezeten onderdanen van derde landen (PbEU L 16) te verkrijgen;
d. de persoon die anderszins op grond van bepalingen van verdragen of besluiten van volkenrechtelijke organisaties geen inburgeringsplicht als bedoeld in artikel 7 kan worden opgelegd.
3. De inburgeringsplichtige die beschikt over een bij of krachtens algemene maatregel van bestuur aangewezen diploma, certificaat of ander document, waaruit blijkt dat hij reeds beschikt over een deel van de vaardigheden en kennis, bedoeld in artikel 7, is vrijgesteld van de verplichting om dat deel van die kennis of vaardigheden te verwerven.
4. Bij of krachtens algemene maatregel van bestuur kunnen regels worden gesteld omtrent:
a. verdere gehele of gedeeltelijke vrijstelling van de inburgeringsplicht;
b. het verblijf, bedoeld in het eerste lid, onderdeel b.
5. Onze Minister kan beleidsregels vaststellen omtrent de toepassing van het tweede lid, onderdeel d.

Artikel 6
1. Onze Minister ontheft de inburgeringsplichtige van de inburgeringsplicht, indien:
a. de inburgeringsplichtige heeft aangetoond door een psychische of lichamelijke belemmering, dan wel een verstandelijke handicap, blijvend niet in staat te zijn het inburgeringsexamen te behalen;

b. hij op grond van door de inburgeringsplichtige aantoonbaar geleverde inspanningen tot het oordeel komt dat het voor de inburgeringsplichtige redelijkerwijs niet mogelijk is aan de inburgeringsplicht te voldoen.
2. Bij of krachtens algemene maatregel van bestuur kan worden voorzien in:
a. verdere ontheffing van de inburgeringsplicht, en
b. nadere regels omtrent de toepassing van het eerste lid.
3. Voor het in behandeling nemen van een aanvraag van een ontheffing als bedoeld in het eerste of tweede lid, dan wel voor een medisch onderzoek ten behoeve van de ontheffing, kan een bij ministeriële regeling te bepalen bedrag worden vastgesteld, dat de inburgeringsplichtige is verschuldigd. Onder de inburgeringsplichtige, bedoeld in de eerste zin, wordt mede verstaan de inburgeringsplichtige, bedoeld in artikel X, tweede lid, van de Wet van 13 september 2012 tot wijziging van de Wet inburgering en enkele wetten in verband met de versterking van de eigen verantwoordelijkheid van de inburgeringsplichtige (Stb. 2012, 430), die een ontheffing aanvraagt op grond van artikel 6, zoals dit artikel luidde op 31 december 2012.

Artikel 7
1. De inburgeringsplichtige verwerft binnen drie jaar mondelinge en schriftelijke vaardigheden in de Nederlandse taal op ten minste het niveau A2 van het Europese Raamwerk voor Moderne Vreemde Talen en kennis van de Nederlandse samenleving.
2. De inburgeringsplichtige heeft aan de inburgeringsplicht voldaan indien hij:
a. het door Onze Minister vastgestelde examen heeft behaald, of
b. een diploma, certificaat of ander document, bedoeld in artikel 5, eerste lid, onderdeel c, heeft behaald.
3. Onze Minister verlengt de in het eerste lid bedoelde termijn:
a. indien de inburgeringsplichtige aannemelijk maakt dat hem geen verwijt treft terzake van het niet voldoen aan de inburgeringsplicht, of
b. eenmalig met ten hoogste twee jaren, indien aantoonbaar een alfabetiseringscursus wordt of is gevolgd voor het verstrijken van die termijn.
4. Bij of krachtens algemene maatregel van bestuur worden regels gesteld omtrent:
a. de verdere verlenging van de termijn, bedoeld in het eerste lid, en de toepassing van het derde lid;
b. het afnemen van het examen;
c. de inhoud en vormgeving van het examen;
d. de ter zake van het examen verschuldigde kosten;
e. de identificatie van de persoon die aan het examen deelneemt;

f. de examencommissie, en
g. het diploma.

Vreemdelingenwet 2000, 23 November 2000[11]

Hoofdstuk 3. Verblijf

Afdeling 1. Rechtmatig verblijf

Artikel 8
De vreemdeling heeft in Nederland uitsluitend rechtmatig verblijf:
a. op grond van een verblijfsvergunning voor bepaalde tijd als bedoeld in artikel 14;
b. op grond van een verblijfsvergunning voor onbepaalde tijd als bedoeld in artikel 20;
c. op grond van een verblijfsvergunning voor bepaalde tijd als bedoeld in artikel 28;
d. op grond van een verblijfsvergunning voor onbepaalde tijd als bedoeld in artikel 33;
e. als gemeenschapsonderdaan zolang deze onderdaan verblijf houdt op grond van een regeling krachtens het Verdrag tot oprichting van de Europese Gemeenschap dan wel de Overeenkomst betreffende de Europese Economische Ruimte;
f. in afwachting van de beslissing op een aanvraag tot het verlenen van de verblijfsvergunning, bedoeld in de artikelen 14 en 28, terwijl bij of krachtens deze wet dan wel op grond van een rechterlijke beslissing uitzetting van de aanvrager achterwege dient te blijven totdat op de aanvraag is beslist;
g. in afwachting van de beslissing op een aanvraag tot het verlenen van de verblijfsvergunning, bedoeld in de artikelen 20 en 33, of tot het verlengen van de geldigheidsduur van de verblijfsvergunning, bedoeld in de artikelen 14 en 28, of een wijziging ervan, terwijl bij of krachtens deze wet of op grond van een rechterlijke beslissing uitzetting van de aanvrager achterwege dient te blijven totdat op de aanvraag is beslist;
h. in afwachting van de beslissing op een bezwaarschrift of een beroepschrift, terwijl bij of krachtens deze wet of op grond van een rechterlijke beslissing uitzetting van de aanvrager achterwege dient te blijven totdat op het bezwaarschrift of het beroepschrift is beslist;

11 Vreemdelingenwet 2000 of 23 November 2000, available at http://wetten.overheid.nl/BWBR0011823 [last accessed on 11 January 2014].

i. gedurende de vrije termijn, bedoeld in artikel 12, zolang het verblijf van de vreemdeling bij of krachtens artikel 12 is toegestaan;
j. indien tegen de uitzetting beletselen bestaan als bedoeld in artikel 64;
k. gedurende de periode waarin de vreemdeling door Onze Minister in de gelegenheid wordt gesteld aangifte te doen van overtreding van artikel 273f van het Wetboek van Strafrecht;
l. indien de vreemdeling verblijfsrecht ontleent aan het Associatiebesluit 1/80 van de Associatieraad EEG/Turkije;
m. na afwijzing van de aanvraag tot het verlenen van een verblijfsvergunning op grond van artikel 30, eerste lid, onderdeel a, terwijl hij in afwachting is van de feitelijke overdracht naar een verantwoordelijke lidstaat in de zin van de Dublinverordening.
[...]

Afdeling 3. De verblijfsvergunning regulier

Paragraaf 1. De verblijfsvergunning voor bepaalde tijd

Artikel 14
1. Onze Minister is bevoegd:
a. de aanvraag tot het verlenen van een verblijfsvergunning voor bepaalde tijd in te willigen, af te wijzen dan wel niet in behandeling te nemen;
b. de aanvraag tot het verlengen van de geldigheidsduur ervan in te willigen, af te wijzen dan wel niet in behandeling te nemen;
c. een verblijfsvergunning voor bepaalde tijd op aanvraag of ambtshalve te wijzigen wegens veranderde omstandigheden;
d. een verblijfsvergunning voor bepaalde tijd in te trekken;
e. ambtshalve een verblijfsvergunning voor bepaalde tijd te verlenen dan wel de geldigheidsduur ervan te verlengen.
2. Onze Minister verleent de houder van een geldige machtiging tot voorlopig verblijf binnen twee weken nadat deze zich overeenkomstig artikel 54, eerste lid, onder e, heeft aangemeld, ambtshalve een verblijfsvergunning voor bepaalde tijd onder dezelfde beperking als die waaronder de machtiging tot voorlopig verblijf is verleend.
3. Een verblijfsvergunning voor bepaalde tijd wordt verleend onder beperkingen, verband houdende met het doel waarvoor het verblijf is toegestaan. Aan de vergunning kunnen voorschriften worden verbonden. Bij of krachtens algemene maatregel van bestuur kunnen regels worden gesteld over de ambtshalve verlening, wijziging en verlenging, de beperkingen en de voorschriften.

4. De verblijfsvergunning voor bepaalde tijd wordt verleend voor ten hoogste vijf achtereenvolgende jaren. Bij algemene maatregel van bestuur worden regels gesteld over de geldigheidsduur van de verblijfsvergunning en de verlenging van de geldigheidsduur van de verblijfsvergunning.

Artikel 15
In de algemene maatregel van bestuur, bedoeld in artikel 14, tweede lid, wordt bepaald, dat de verblijfsvergunning voor bepaalde tijd, bedoeld in artikel 14, kan worden verleend onder een beperking verband houdend met verblijf als familie- of gezinslid aan gezinsleden van Nederlanders en vreemdelingen die rechtmatig verblijven als bedoeld in artikel 8, onder a tot en met e en l.

Artikel 16
1. Een aanvraag tot het verlenen van een verblijfsvergunning voor bepaalde tijd als bedoeld in artikel 14 kan worden afgewezen indien:
a. de vreemdeling niet beschikt over een geldige machtiging tot voorlopig verblijf die overeenkomt met het verblijfsdoel waarvoor de verblijfsvergunning is aangevraagd;
b. de vreemdeling niet beschikt over een geldig document voor grensoverschrijding;
c. de vreemdeling niet zelfstandig en duurzaam beschikt over voldoende middelen van bestaan dan wel, indien de persoon bij wie de vreemdeling wil verblijven, niet zelfstandig en duurzaam beschikt over voldoende middelen van bestaan;
d. de vreemdeling een gevaar vormt voor de openbare orde of nationale veiligheid;
e. de vreemdeling niet bereid is om medewerking te verlenen aan een medisch onderzoek naar een ziekte aangewezen bij of krachtens de Infectieziektewet, ter bescherming van de volksgezondheid of een medische behandeling tegen een dergelijke ziekte te ondergaan;
f. de vreemdeling voor een werkgever arbeid verricht, zonder dat aan de Wet arbeid vreemdelingen is voldaan;
g. de vreemdeling niet voldoet aan de beperking, verband houdende met het doel waarvoor hij wil verblijven;
h. de vreemdeling, die niet behoort tot een der categorieën, bedoeld in artikel 17, eerste lid, na verkrijging van rechtmatig verblijf in Nederland inburgeringsplichtig zou zijn op grond van de artikelen 3 en 5 van de Wet inburgering en niet beschikt over kennis op basisniveau van de Nederlandse taal en de Nederlandse maatschappij;
i. de vreemdeling onjuiste gegevens heeft verstrekt dan wel gegevens heeft achtergehouden terwijl die gegevens tot afwijzing van een eerdere aanvraag

tot het verlenen, verlengen of wijzigen van een visum of een verblijfsvergunning hebben geleid of zouden hebben geleid;
j. de vreemdeling in Nederland verblijf heeft gehouden, anders dan op grond van artikel 8.
k. ten behoeve van het verblijf van de vreemdeling geen verklaring van een referent is overgelegd als bedoeld in artikel 2a, eerste lid.
2. Bij of krachtens algemene maatregel van bestuur kunnen regels worden gesteld over de toepassing van de gronden, bedoeld in het eerste lid.
3. Het eerste lid, onder h, is niet van toepassing op de vreemdeling die de Surinaamse nationaliteit bezit en die met bij ministeriële regeling vastgestelde bescheiden heeft aangetoond in Suriname of Nederland lager onderwijs in de Nederlandse taal te hebben gevolgd.

Artikel 16a
1. De aanvraag tot het wijzigen van een verblijfsvergunning voor bepaalde tijd als bedoeld in artikel 14 kan worden afgewezen op de gronden, bedoeld in artikel 16, eerste lid, onder b tot en met g en k, alsmede indien de vreemdeling het examen, bedoeld in artikel 7, tweede lid, onderdeel a, van de Wet inburgering, of een diploma, certificaat of ander document, bedoeld in artikel 5, eerste lid, onderdeel c, van die wet, niet heeft behaald.
2. Bij of krachtens algemene maatregel van bestuur kunnen regels worden gesteld over de toepassing van de gronden, bedoeld in het eerste lid.
[...]

Paragraaf 2. De verblijfsvergunning voor onbepaalde tijd

Artikel 20
1. Onze Minister is bevoegd:
a. de aanvraag tot het verlenen of tot het wijzigen van een verblijfsvergunning voor onbepaalde tijd in te willigen, af te wijzen dan wel niet in behandeling te nemen;
b. een verblijfsvergunning voor onbepaalde tijd in te trekken dan wel te wijzigen.
2. Een verblijfsvergunning voor onbepaalde tijd wordt niet onder beperkingen verleend. Aan de vergunning worden geen voorschriften verbonden.

Artikel 21
1. Ter uitvoering van artikel 8, tweede lid, van de richtlijn nr. 2003/109/EG van de Raad van de Europese Unie van 25 november 2003 betreffende de status van langdurig ingezeten onderdanen van derde landen (PbEU 2004, L16) kan

de aanvraag tot het verlenen of wijzigen van een verblijfsvergunning voor onbepaalde tijd als bedoeld in artikel 20 slechts worden afgewezen, indien de vreemdeling:
a. niet gedurende vijf jaren ononderbroken en direct voorafgaande aan de aanvraag rechtmatig verblijf heeft gehad als bedoeld in artikel 8;
b. in de periode, bedoeld onder a, verblijfsrecht van tijdelijke aard heeft gehad, dan wel een formeel beperkt verblijfsrecht of een verblijfsrecht als werknemer van een dienstverlener in het kader van grensoverschrijdende diensten of als verlener van grensoverschrijdende diensten heeft gehad;
c. in de periode, bedoeld onder a, zes of meer achtereenvolgende maanden of in totaal tien of meer maanden buiten Nederland heeft verbleven;
d. al of niet tezamen met het gezinslid bij wie hij verblijft, niet zelfstandig en duurzaam beschikt over voldoende middelen van bestaan;
e. bij onherroepelijk geworden rechterlijk vonnis is veroordeeld wegens een misdrijf waartegen een gevangenisstraf van drie jaren of meer is bedreigd, dan wel hem terzake de maatregel, bedoeld in artikel 37a van het Wetboek van Strafrecht, is opgelegd;
f. een gevaar vormt voor de nationale veiligheid;
g. niet beschikt over een toereikende ziektekostenverzekering voor hemzelf en de te zijnen laste komende gezinsleden,
h. onjuiste gegevens heeft verstrekt dan wel gegevens heeft achtergehouden terwijl die gegevens tot afwijzing van de aanvraag tot het verlenen, wijzigen of verlengen zouden hebben geleid;
i. rechtmatig verblijf heeft als bedoeld in artikel 8, onderdeel c of d, of in afwachting is van een definitieve beslissing tot het verlenen of verlengen van de geldigheidsduur van een verblijfsvergunning als bedoeld in de artikelen 28 of 33; of
j. een bijzondere geprivilegieerde status bezit dan wel heeft bezeten in de periode van vijf jaren direct voorafgaande aan de aanvraag;
k. het examen, bedoeld in artikel 7, tweede lid, onderdeel a, van de Wet inburgering, of een diploma, certificaat of ander document, bedoeld in artikel 5, eerste lid, onderdeel c, van die wet, niet heeft behaald.
2. Bij of krachtens algemene maatregel van bestuur kunnen regels worden gesteld over de gronden, bedoeld in het eerste lid.
3. Tenzij de vergunning is verleend met toepassing van artikel 21a, wordt op het document, bedoeld in artikel 9, de aantekening "EG-langdurig ingezetene" geplaatst.

Artikel 21a
1. Ter uitvoering van artikel 13 van de richtlijn nr. 2003/109/EG van de Raad van de Europese Unie van 25 november 2003 betreffende de status van langdurig

ingezeten onderdanen van derde landen (PbEU 2004, L16) wordt de aanvraag tot het verlenen van een verblijfsvergunning voor onbepaalde tijd als bedoeld in artikel 20 niet afgewezen op de grond, bedoeld in artikel 21, eerste lid, onder d, indien:
a. de vreemdeling gedurende een tijdvak van tien aaneengesloten jaren rechtmatig verblijf als bedoeld in artikel 8, onder a, of l, heeft gehad, of
b. de vreemdeling als minderjarige onder een beperking verband houdend met gezinshereniging rechtmatig verblijf heeft gehad, sindsdien zijn hoofdverblijf niet buiten Nederland heeft verplaatst en inmiddels 18 jaar is, tenzij de gezinsband werd verbroken binnen een jaar na verlening van de verblijfvergunning, bedoeld in artikel 14.
2. Indien de vreemdeling in Nederland is geboren dan wel reeds voor zijn vierde levensjaar in Nederland verbleef en sindsdien zijn hoofdverblijf niet buiten Nederland heeft verplaatst en inmiddels 18 jaar is, kan de aanvraag slechts worden afgewezen op grond van artikel 21, eerste lid, onder e en f. In afwijking van artikel 21, eerste lid, onder a, behoeft het rechtmatig verblijf niet aaneengesloten te zijn. De aanvraag kan slechts op grond van artikel 21, eerste lid, onder e, worden afgewezen, indien de vreemdeling bij onherroepelijk geworden rechterlijk vonnis is veroordeeld tot een gevangenisstraf van meer dan 60 maanden wegens handel in verdovende middelen.
3. Bij of krachtens algemene maatregel van bestuur kunnen andere gevallen dan bedoeld in het eerste en tweede lid worden aangewezen waarin een verblijfsvergunning voor onbepaalde tijd als bedoeld in artikel 20 kan worden verleend.

Artikel 22
1. De verblijfsvergunning voor onbepaalde tijd als bedoeld in artikel 20 kan worden ingetrokken of gewijzigd, indien:
a. de vreemdeling een aaneengesloten periode van twaalf maanden of langer buiten het grondgebied van de staten die partij zijn bij het Verdrag tot oprichting van de Europese Gemeenschap, dan wel zes jaar of langer buiten Nederland heeft verbleven;
b. de verblijfsvergunning op frauduleuze wijze is verkregen;
c. de vreemdeling een actuele en ernstige bedreiging voor de openbare orde of de nationale veiligheid vormt.
2. De verblijfsvergunning wordt ingetrokken, indien de vreemdeling langdurig ingezetene is geworden in een andere staat die partij is bij het Verdrag tot oprichting van de Europese Gemeenschap.
3. Bij of krachtens algemene maatregel van bestuur kunnen nadere regels worden gesteld over de toepassing van de gronden, bedoeld in het eerste lid.
[...]

Afdeling 4. De verblijfsvergunning asiel

Paragraaf 1. De verblijfsvergunning voor bepaalde tijd

Artikel 28
1. Onze Minister is bevoegd:
a. de aanvraag tot het verlenen van een verblijfsvergunning voor bepaalde tijd in te willigen, af te wijzen dan wel niet in behandeling te nemen;
b. de aanvraag tot het verlengen van de geldigheidsduur ervan in te willigen, af te wijzen dan wel niet in behandeling te nemen;
c. een verblijfsvergunning voor bepaalde tijd in te trekken;
d. ambtshalve een verblijfsvergunning voor bepaalde tijd te verlenen aan de houder van een geldige machtiging tot voorlopig verblijf die voldoet aan de in artikel 29, tweede lid, gestelde voorwaarden.
2. De verblijfsvergunning voor bepaalde tijd wordt verleend voor ten hoogste vijf achtereenvolgende jaren. Bij algemene maatregel van bestuur kunnen de gevallen worden aangewezen waarin de verblijfsvergunning voor minder dan vijf achtereenvolgende jaren wordt verleend. Daarbij kunnen regels worden gesteld over de geldigheidsduur van de verblijfsvergunning en over de verlenging ervan.
3. De verblijfsvergunning wordt ambtshalve verleend binnen twee weken nadat de houder van een geldige machtiging tot voorlopig verblijf zich overeenkomstig artikel 54, eerste lid, onder e, heeft aangemeld.

Artikel 29
1. Een verblijfsvergunning voor bepaalde tijd als bedoeld in artikel 28 kan worden verleend aan de vreemdeling:
a. die verdragsvluchteling is; of
b. die aannemelijk heeft gemaakt dat hij gegronde redenen heeft om aan te nemen dat hij bij uitzetting een reëel risico loopt om te worden onderworpen aan:
1°. doodstraf of executie;
2°. folteringen, onmenselijke of vernederende behandelingen of bestraffingen; of
3°. ernstige en individuele bedreiging van het leven of de persoon van een burger als gevolg van willekeurig geweld in het kader van een internationaal of binnenlands gewapend conflict.

Artikel 30
1. Een aanvraag tot het verlenen van een verblijfsvergunning voor bepaalde tijd als bedoeld in artikel 28 wordt afgewezen indien:

a. een ander land, partij bij het Vluchtelingenverdrag ingevolge een verdrag of een dit land en Nederland bindend besluit van een volkenrechtelijke organisatie verantwoordelijk is voor de behandeling van de aanvraag;
b. de vreemdeling reeds rechtmatig verblijf heeft, als bedoeld in artikel 8, onder a tot en met e of l;
c. de vreemdeling eerder een aanvraag voor verlening van een verblijfsvergunning heeft ingediend waarop nog niet onherroepelijk is beslist en hij op grond van die aanvraag rechtmatig verblijf heeft als bedoeld in artikel 8 onder f, g en h;
d. de vreemdeling in een andere lidstaat van de Europese Unie, in een staat die partij is bij de Overeenkomst betreffende de Europese Economische Ruimte of in Zwitserland internationale bescherming geniet in de zin van artikel 2, eerste lid onder a van de kwalificatierichtlijn, dan wel een gelijkwaardige status bezit op basis van het Vluchtelingenverdrag of artikel 3 van het Europees Verdrag voor de Rechten van de Mens en de fundamentele vrijheden; of
e. de vreemdeling op grond van een verdragsverplichting tussen Nederland en een ander land zal worden overgedragen aan dat land van eerder verblijf, terwijl dat land partij is bij het Vluchtelingenverdrag, het Verdrag tot bescherming van de rechten van de mens en de fundamentele vrijheden (Trb. 1951, 154) en het Verdrag tegen foltering en andere wrede, onmenselijke of onterende behandeling of bestraffing (Trb. 1985, 69), dan wel zich anderszins heeft verplicht artikel 33 van het Vluchtelingenverdrag, artikel 3 van het Verdrag tot bescherming van de rechten van de mens en de fundamentele vrijheden en artikel 3 van het Verdrag tegen foltering en andere wrede onmenselijke of onterende behandeling of bestraffing, na te leven.
2. Het eerste lid, onder b, is niet van toepassing, indien naar aanleiding van een aanvraag tot het verlenen van de verblijfsvergunning, bedoeld in artikel 28, ambtshalve de verblijfsvergunning, bedoeld in artikel 14, is verleend.
3. Bij of krachtens algemene maatregel van bestuur worden regels gesteld met betrekking tot het eerste lid, onder d en e.
[...]

Paragraaf 2. De verblijfsvergunning voor onbepaalde tijd

Artikel 33
Onze Minister is bevoegd:
a. de aanvraag tot het verlenen van een verblijfsvergunning voor onbepaalde tijd in te willigen, af te wijzen dan wel niet in behandeling te nemen;
b. een verleende verblijfsvergunning voor onbepaalde tijd in te trekken.
[...]

Vreemdelingenbesluit 2000, 23 November 2000[12]

Artikel 3.33
1. Onverminderd artikel 3.31 kan de verblijfsvergunning voor bepaalde tijd, bedoeld in artikel 14 van de Wet, onder een beperking verband houdend met het verrichten van arbeid in loondienst als geestelijk voorganger of godsdienstleraar slechts worden verleend, indien de vreemdeling tevens schriftelijk verklaart ermee bekend te zijn dat:
a. slechts verblijf wordt toegestaan voor het verrichten van werkzaamheden als geestelijk voorganger of godsdienstleraar ten behoeve van de met name te noemen groepering;
b. het verblijf slechts kan worden toegestaan voor de duur van de werkzaamheden;
c. hij na beëindiging daarvan Nederland dient te verlaten, en
d. het hem niet is toegestaan om gedurende zijn verblijf in Nederland werkzaamheden van andere aard te verrichten.
2. Het model van de verklaring wordt bij ministeriële regeling vastgesteld.
[...]

Artikel 3.71
1. De aanvraag tot het verlenen van de verblijfsvergunning voor bepaalde tijd, bedoeld in artikel 14 van de Wet, wordt afgewezen, indien de vreemdeling niet beschikt over een geldige machtiging tot voorlopig verblijf.
Van het vereiste van een geldige machtiging tot verblijf is, op grond van artikel 17, eerste lid, onder g, van de Wet, vrijgesteld de vreemdeling:
a. [vervallen;]
b. van twaalf jaar of jonger, die in Nederland is geboren en naar het oordeel van Onze Minister feitelijk is blijven behoren tot het gezin van een ouder die
1°. sedert het moment van geboorte van de vreemdeling rechtmatig verblijf in Nederland heeft op grond van artikel 8, onder a tot en met e, dan wel l, van de Wet of als Nederlander, of
2°. op het moment van de geboorte van de vreemdeling rechtmatig verblijf in Nederland had op grond van artikel 8, onder f tot en met k, van de Wet en die sedertdien aansluitend rechtmatig verblijf op grond van artikel 8, onder a tot en met e, dan wel l, van de Wet heeft, voor zover geen van beiden het hoofdverblijf buiten Nederland heeft verplaatst;

12 Vreemdelingenbesluit 2000, available at http://wetten.overheid.nl/BWBR0011825 [last accessed on 25 January 2014].

c. die in Nederland verblijft op grond van een geprivilegieerde status als gezinslid van een in Nederland geaccrediteerd personeelslid van een buitenlandse diplomatieke of consulaire post die zelf in aanmerking komt voor de verblijfsvergunning voor onbepaalde tijd, bedoeld in artikel 21 van de Wet;
d. die ten minste zeven jaren werkzaam is of is geweest op een Nederlands zeeschip of een mijnbouwinstallatie op het continentaal plat;
e. die in aanmerking komt voor een verblijfsvergunning op grond van Besluit 1/80 van de Associatieraad EEG-Turkije betreffende de ontwikkeling van de Associatie of van wie uitzetting in strijd zou zijn met de op 12 september 1963 te Ankara gesloten Overeenkomst waarbij een associatie tot stand wordt gebracht tussen de Europese Economische Gemeenschap en Turkije (Trb. 1964, 217), het op 23 november 1970 te Brussel tot stand gekomen Aanvullend Protocol bij die overeenkomst (Trb. 1971, 70) of dat Besluit nr. 1/80;
f. [vervallen;]
g. die in Nederland verblijft, bij de rechtbank Den Haag een verzoek heeft ingediend tot vaststelling van zijn Nederlanderschap dat naar het oordeel van Onze Minister niet klaarblijkelijk van elke grond ontbloot is;
h. die tijdelijke bescherming heeft en in aanmerking komt voor de verblijfsvergunning voor bepaalde tijd, bedoeld in artikel 14 van de wet, onder een beperking verband houdend met seizoenarbeid, arbeid in loondienst, arbeid als kennismigrant of arbeid als zelfstandige;
i. die houder is van een verblijfsvergunning voor onderzoekers in de zin van richtlijn 2005/71/EG afgegeven door een andere staat die Partij is bij het Verdrag betreffende de werking van de Europese Unie, dan wel de echtgenoot, partner of het minderjarig kind is van die houder, tenzij sprake is van gezinsvorming;
j. [vervallen;]
k. die minderjarig is, schoolgaand is en drie jaar ononderbroken hoofdverblijf in Nederland heeft en een aanvraag heeft ingediend tot het verlenen van een verblijfsvergunning voor bepaalde tijd als bedoeld in artikel 14 van de Wet, onder een beperking verband houdend met gezinshereniging bij een Nederlander of een hoofdpersoon met rechtmatig verblijf, als bedoeld in artikel 8, onder a tot en met e dan wel l, van de Wet;
l. van wie uitzetting in strijd met artikel 8 van het Verdrag tot bescherming van de rechten van de mens en de fundamentele vrijheden zou zijn.
3. Het tweede lid, met uitzondering van onderdeel h, is niet van toepassing op de vreemdeling die als geestelijk voorganger of godsdienstleraar wil verblijven.

Kieswet, 28 September 1989[13]

Artikel B 3
1. De leden van de gemeenteraden worden gekozen door degenen die op de dag van de kandidaatstelling ingezetenen zijn van de gemeente en op de dag van de stemming de leeftijd van achttien jaar hebben bereikt.
2. Zij die geen onderdaan van een lidstaat van de Europese Unie zijn, dienen om kiesgerechtigd te zijn op de dag van de kandidaatstelling tevens te voldoen aan de vereisten dat:
a. zij rechtmatig in Nederland verblijven op grond van artikel 8, onder a, b, c, d, e of l, van de Vreemdelingenwet 2000 of op grond van een verdrag tussen een internationale organisatie en de Staat der Nederlanden inzake de zetel van deze organisatie in Nederland, en
b. zij onmiddellijk voorafgaand aan de dag van de kandidaatstelling gedurende een onafgebroken periode van ten minste vijf jaren ingezetene van Nederland waren en beschikten over een verblijfsrecht als bedoeld onder a, dan wel op grond van artikel 3 of artikel 6 van de Wet toelating en uitzetting BES.

Ambtenarenwet of 12 December 1929[14]

Artikel 125quater
Het bevoegd gezag van ambtenaren die door of vanwege het rijk, de provincies, de gemeenten of de waterschappen zijn aangesteld,
a. voert een integriteitsbeleid dat is gericht op het bevorderen van goed ambtelijk handelen en dat in ieder geval aandacht besteedt aan het bevorderen van integriteitsbewustzijn en aan het voorkomen van misbruik van bevoegdheden, belangenverstrengeling en discriminatie;
[...]

Jurisprudence

Case 1

An imam sought legal permission to extend his stay in the Netherlands for a limited period of time on the basis that he worked as a teacher of religion. The

13 Kieswet, available at http://wetten.overheid.nl/BWBR0004627 [last accessed on 2 June 2014].

14 Ambtenarenwet, available at http://wetten.overheid.nl/BWBR0001947 [last accessed on 2 June 2014].

application was rejected however. The defendant, i.e. the Ministry of Immigration and Integration, based the decision on the ultraorthodox and radical character of the salafist foundation, to which the imam was affiliated. This, in the defendant's opinion, posed a threat to democratic order and national security. According to the court, the radical convictions expressed by the imam and his passive attitude towards the radical activities undertaken in the organisation were insufficient arguments to prove the potential threat he could pose to national security. The court did however admit they could possibly contribute to the radicalisation of the mosque's attenders. It was emphasised that the respondent had not been prosecuted for any acts of this nature in the past. The court held that the documents and analyses on which the Ministry based its argument did not provide sufficient evidence to refuse the imam permission to stay in the Netherlands. (Rechtbank 's-Gravenhage, 2 November 2006, ECLI:NL:RBSGR:2006:AZ1371)[15]

Case 2

An applicant of Iranian origin sought to extend his permission to stay in the Netherlands for a limited period of time, in the form of asylum. The applicant claimed that due to his conversion to the faith of Jehova's Witnesses (and thereby the fact that he was no longer a Muslim), his return to Iran would pose a threat to his safety. Moreover, his religious convictions involved proselytism which is forbidden in Iran. The application was refused by the relevant authorities who claimed the applicant could limit his preaching activity. Nevertheless, the Court held that it could not be expected that the applicant would abandon proselytism, which formed a crucial element of his faith, and considered the former decision ungrounded. (Rechtbank 's-Gravenhage, 11 February 2011, ECLI:NL:RBSGR:2011:BQ4669)[16]

15 Available at http://uitspraken.rechtspraak.nl/inziendocument?id=ECLI:NL:RBSGR:2006:AZ1371 [last accessed on 10 February 2014].

16 Available at http://uitspraken.rechtspraak.nl/inziendocument?id=ECLI:NL:RBSGR:2011:BQ4669 [last accessed on 1 March 2014].

CHAPTER 5

Mosques and Prayer Houses

The general rules concerning the establishment of mosques and prayer houses in the Netherlands have been defined at a national level, while the practical, detailed policy, as well as the implementation of these rules and the execution of national law in practice, is subject to local authorities' competences.[1] This also concerns the opportunity to subsidise certain socio-cultural activities of Islamic communities. Here one can observe differences between particular municipalities.[2] The general right to establish mosques in the Netherlands[3] is interpreted on the basis of Art. 6 of the Constitution, and has been defined in terms of the freedom of religion.[4]

Until 1975, issues concerning the state funding of church buildings were regulated by the Act on Subsidies for Church Building (*Wet premie kerkenbouw*) of 1962. This Act guaranteed 'traditional' Dutch religious communities the opportunity to access public subsidies. In the 1970s however, the presence of other religious communities (Muslims in particular) was becoming increasingly visible and active. The regulation of 1976 redefined the principles of financing churches. Nevertheless, it was not until 1981 that the position of Muslims and Christians was equated through the introduction of (temporary) solutions. This allowed Islamic communities to receive state subsidies for the construction of mosques.[5] Just after this regulation expired in 1983, a special working group (*Werkgroep-Waardenburg*) was established. Its purpose was to analyse the legal

---

1 See Koning de, 'Netherlands', p. 248.

2 See Douwes, Koning de, Boender, *Nederlandse moslims …*, p. 88.

3 The first mosque was built in the Netherlands (The Hague) in 1955. See Bernts, Jong de, Yar, 'Een religieuze atlas van Nederland', p. 113.

4 This reasoning was used in the response (2013-0000155248) of the Ministry of Social Affairs and Employment to the question by a deputy of the PVV, Joran van Klaveren, *Antwoorden kamervragen bouw moskee in Groningen*, ref. no. 2013Z18928, 13 November 2013, available at http://www.rijksoverheid.nl/bestanden/documenten-en-publicaties/kamerstukken/2013/11/13/antwoorden-kamervragen-bouw-moskee-in-groningen/antwoorden-kamervragen-bouw-moskee-in-groningen.pdf [last accessed on 2 January 2014]. See also the response of the Ministry to the question by Geert Wilders and Joran van Klaveren (PVV), ref. no. 2013Z17469, 11 October 2013. One of the questions in both documents concerned the conditions of funding the mosques, particularly the presence of foreign financial sources. Regarding Art. 6 of the Constitution see also section 1.1.

5 Schwitters, Robert J.S., *Recht en samenleving in verandering* (Deventer: Kluwer 2000), p. 246.

possibility of incorporating minority communities into the system of state subsidies. In its final justification, the commission backed its position by highlighting the multi-religious structure of Dutch society. The subsequent establishment of the new Constitution broke the financial links between the state and religious communities in the name of the principle of state neutrality and the separation of church and state.[6]

In 1988 the Monuments Act (Monumentenwet, hereafter Mw) was introduced, which obliged the state to support the cultural heritage of the nation.[7] According to the Mw, as amended, such cultural elements are also embodied by sacred buildings, which therefore require state protection and financial support for their maintenance and renovation.[8] Here one should note that the legislator indicates that such a building should be owned by a 'religious community' or any other community based on religious or worldview grounds (Art. 1e). Due to this definition, other forms of organisation adopted by Islamic communities have also been embraced by the Mw.

A significant statement regarding the financial support of religious buildings was also placed in the Municipal Act (Gemeentewet, hereafter Gw) in 1992. Art. 220d §1c of the Gw incorporates the notion that real property owned by religious communities and used for public religious worship or public assemblies of a worldview nature is not subject to taxation. In such cases at least 70% of a building's space should be used for religious purposes, according to the law.[9]

Monumentenwet, 23 December 1988[10]

Artikel 1
In deze wet en de daarop berustende bepalingen wordt verstaan onder:
a. Onze minister: Onze Minister van Onderwijs, Cultuur en Wetenschap;

6 The legal opportunities for state subsidies for the building of mosques were subject to broad parliamentary debate, which led to the establishment of advisory commissions. However, the debate did not contribute to any new legal provisions concerning state financial support for mosques. See Brand, Charlotte, '"Moorse minaretten" op kosten van de staat?', in Baalen, Carla C. van et. al. (eds.), *Jaarboek Parlementaire Geschiedenis 2005. God in de Nederlandse Politiek* (Den Haag, 2005) pp. 76–88.

7 The conditions of such subsidies are subject to implementing regulations (Art. 34 of the Mw).

8 Bijsterveld van, *Godsdienstvrijheid ...*, pp. 82–83.

9 See Bijsterveld van, *Godsdienstvrijheid ...*, p. 84.

10 Monumentenwet, available at http://wetten.overheid.nl/BWBR0004471 [last accessed on 21 January 2014].

b. monumenten:
1. vervaardigde zaken welke van algemeen belang zijn wegens hun schoonheid, hun betekenis voor de wetenschap of hun cultuurhistorische waarde;
2. terreinen welke van algemeen belang zijn wegens daar aanwezige zaken als bedoeld onder 1;
[...]
e. kerkelijke monumenten: onroerende monumenten welke eigendom zijn van een kerkgenootschap, een zelfstandig onderdeel daarvan, een lichaam waarin kerkgenootschappen zijn verenigd, of van een ander genootschap op geestelijke grondslag en welke uitsluitend of voor een overwegend deel worden gebruikt voor het gezamenlijk belijden van de godsdienst of levensovertuiging;

Artikel 2
1. Bij de toepassing van deze wet wordt rekening gehouden met het gebruik van het monument.
2. Met betrekking tot een kerkelijk monument wordt geen beslissing genomen ingevolge deze wet dan na overleg met de eigenaar.
[...]

Artikel 34
1. Onze minister kan subsidie verstrekken ten behoeve van de instandhouding van beschermde monumenten. Onder instandhouding wordt verstaan de onderhoudswerkzaamheden aan een beschermd monument alsmede werkzaamheden die het normale onderhoud te boven gaan en die voor het herstel van het monument noodzakelijk zijn.
2. De subsidie bestaat uit hetzij een vast bedrag per jaar hetzij een percentage van de door Onze minister vast te stellen kosten.
3. Bij of krachtens algemene maatregel van bestuur worden regels gesteld met betrekking tot het verstrekken van subsidie, bedoeld in het eerste lid. Deze regels kunnen betrekking hebben op:
a. de criteria op grond waarvan subsidie kan worden verstrekt;
b. de wijze waarop het subsidiebedrag wordt bepaald;
c. de vaststelling van een subsidieplafond;
d. de aanvraag van een subsidie;
e. de voorwaarden waaronder de subsidie wordt verleend;
f. de verplichtingen van de subsidie-ontvanger;
g. de vaststelling van de subsidie;
h. de betaling en terugvordering van de subsidie, alsmede het verlenen van voorschotten op de subsidie.

4. Indien bij of krachtens algemene maatregel van bestuur wordt voorzien in een subsidieplafond, worden daarbij regels gesteld omtrent de wijze van verdeling.
5. De voordracht voor een krachtens het derde lid vast te stellen algemene maatregel van bestuur wordt niet eerder gedaan dan vier weken nadat het ontwerp aan beide kamers der Staten-Generaal is overgelegd. Het tijdstip van de overlegging wordt zodanig gekozen dat ten minste drie vierde deel van de termijn buiten een reces van de kamers valt.
6. Onze minister kan tevens subsidie verstrekken in verband met de herbestemming van onroerende monumenten.
7. Bij ministeriële regeling worden regels gesteld met betrekking tot het verstrekken van de subsidie, bedoeld in het zesde lid. De tweede volzin van het derde lid is van toepassing en het vierde lid is van overeenkomstige toepassing.

Gemeentewet, 14 February 1992[11]

Artikel 220d
1. In afwijking in zoverre van artikel 220c wordt bij de bepaling van de heffingsmaatstaf voor de onroerende-zaakbelastingen buiten aanmerking gelaten, voor zover dit niet reeds is geschied bij de bepaling van de in dat artikel bedoelde waarde, de waarde van:
[...]
c. onroerende zaken die in hoofdzaak zijn bestemd voor de openbare eredienst of voor het houden van openbare bezinningssamenkomsten van levensbeschouwelijke aard, een en ander met uitzondering van delen van zodanige onroerende zaken die dienen als woning;
[...]

Jurisprudence

Case 1

When granting permission to build a mosque or a prayer house, the municipality has the right to introduce further regulations and control their implementation with regard e.g. to the selection of the materials used or sound installations (such as the emission and volume of the sound calling for prayer). The munici-

11 Gemeentewet, available at http://wetten.overheid.nl/BWBR0005416 [last accessed on 20 January 2014].

pal authorities are also obliged to consider issues such as the number of parking places that need to be provided. (e.g. Rechtbank Arnhem, 13 December 2007, ECLI:NL:RBARN:2007:BC0280)[12]

---

12 Available at http://uitspraken.rechtspraak.nl/inziendocument?id=ECLI:NL:RBARN:2007:BC0280 [last accessed on 20 January 2014].

CHAPTER 6

Burial and Cemeteries

6.1 Funerals

Issues concerning funerals in accordance with particular non-Christian religious traditions have been broadly discussed in the Netherlands since the early 1970s, primarily with reference to Islam and Hinduism.[1] The issues regarding the disposal of the corpse and burial practices in the Netherlands are defined in the Corpse Disposal Act (Wet op de Lijkbezorging, hereafter the WOL), as amended. The law does not explicitly regulate any issues concerning the Islamic tradition of burial and funeral practices (e.g. the required orientation of the body towards Mecca). Nevertheless, in the WOL the needs of Islamic communities have been taken into consideration, i.e. the tradition of burying the deceased preferably within 24 hours of death. Moreover, the WOL has also permitted burial without a coffin,[2] which was not envisaged in the previous law (i.e. the Act of 1869). However, none of the aforementioned rights has been explicitly set out—they can be interpreted from particular provisions (Art. 8, Art. 17). Both of these rights are subject to further legal interpretation in the process of the execution of law. Regarding the Islamic practice of wrapping the body in a shroud and performing the burial without a coffin, in the WOL this right is implied but not explicitly stated. Besides this, the aforementioned exception to the rule of burying the deceased after 36 hours is not automatically guaranteed by the WOL. As stipulated in Art. 16, the deceased must be interred between 36 hours and six days after the death. According to Art. 17, an exception can be made if permission is granted by both the appropriate body representing local authorities (i.e. the Mayor) and the

1 The process of the adjustment of Dutch law to the needs of Islamic communities was initiated in the 1970s and continued throughout the 1980s. See Strijen, Cees R. van, *Lexiplatie: De complete wetgeving toegelicht: Wet op de Lijkbezorging* (Deventer: Kluwer, 2009), pp. 11 and 87–88. See also *Nieuwe bepalingen inzake de lijkbezorging* (*Wet op de lijkbezorging*), Tweede Kamer 1981–1982, 11256, no. 17. Available at http://resourcessgd.kb.nl/SGD/19811982/PDF/SGD_19811982_0002011.pdf [last accessed on 2 June 2014].

2 Koning de, 'Netherlands', p. 251. See also Dessing, Nathal M., *Rituals of Birth, Circumcision, Marriage, and Death Among Muslims in the Netherlands* (Leuven: Peeters, 2001), pp. 168–169, as well as p. 161 and the following pages.

Public Prosecutor (*officier van justitie*).[3] Moreover, Art. 18 clearly states that the (assumed) wish of the deceased should be taken into account, and this should be defined in terms of one's free choice regarding the manner of the burial.

Wet op de Lijkbezorging, 7 March 1991[4]

Artikel 8

1. Op de kist of op een ander omhulsel van het lijk wordt een registratienummer aangebracht, dat correspondeert met het nummer, vermeld op een bijgevoegd document dat tevens de namen, de data van geboorte en overlijden van de overledene dan wel de geslachtsnaam van de doodgeborene bevat, nadat is vastgesteld dat het document betrekking heeft op het lijk.
2. Tot begraving of crematie wordt niet overgegaan dan nadat de houder van de begraafplaats of van het crematorium de overeenkomst heeft vastgesteld tussen het op de kist of het omhulsel vermelde registratienummer en het nummer, vermeld op het document, bedoeld in het eerste lid.
3. Indien er reden is om aan te nemen dat de gegevens op het document dan wel op de kist of het omhulsel niet juist zijn, vindt zo mogelijk de identificatie van het lijk plaats door twee personen die de overledene bij leven hebben gekend, in tegenwoordigheid van de houder van de begraafplaats of het crematorium.

[...]

Artikel 16

Begraving of crematie geschiedt niet eerder dan 36 uren na het overlijden en uiterlijk op de zesde werkdag na het overlijden.

3 In most cases such permission is only a formal matter, which was also stressed in the letter from Minister of the Interior H.F. Dijkstal of 28 January 1998. Moreover, the Islamic definition of 'a full-right human being' refers to a foetus of the age of three months and ten days (in Dutch law—24 weeks), and, therefore, the tradition of burying a foetus also forms an exception under the conditions of the special permissions required to receive a laissez-passer. See *Brief van de Minister Van Binnenlandse Zaken aan de Voorzitter van de Tweede Kamer der Staten-Generaal*, 's-Gravenhage, 28 januari 1998, Tweede Kamer 1997–1998, 25 864, no. 1, available online at https://zoek.officielebekendmakingen.nl/dossier/25864/kst-25864-1?resultIndex=3&sorttype=1&sortorder=4 [last accessed on 19 December 2013].

4 Wet op de Lijkbezorging, available at http://wetten.overheid.nl/BWBR0005009 [last accessed on 2 June 2014].

Artikel 17
1. Na een arts te hebben gehoord kan de burgemeester der gemeente, waar het lijk zich bevindt, voor de begraving of crematie daarvan een andere termijn stellen. Begraving of crematie binnen 36 uur na het overlijden staat hij echter niet toe dan in overeenstemming met de officier van justitie.
2. Van het besluit van de burgemeester staat binnen 24 uur beroep open op Onze Commissaris in de provincie, die daarop onmiddellijk beslist. De Algemene wet bestuursrecht is niet van toepassing.

Artikel 18
1. In de lijkbezorging wordt voorzien door degene, die het in artikel 11 bedoelde verlof aanvraagt, dan wel door degene, die redelijkerwijze geacht kan worden in diens plaats te zijn getreden. De lijkbezorging geschiedt overeenkomstig de wens of de vermoedelijke wens van de overledene, tenzij dat redelijkerwijs niet gevergd kan worden.
2. Onder lijkbezorging wordt voor de toepassing van deze paragraaf begrepen het geven van bestemming aan de as van een gecremeerd lijk.

Jurisprudence

Case 1

A woman declared in writing the wish to be cremated. After her death however, the woman's mother expressed the wish for the burial to be performed in accordance with Islamic practice, which forbids the cremation of the deceased. According to the mother, her daughter was a Muslim and 'carried Islam in her heart'. Moreover, in the mother's opinion, the declaration could not be used as evidence in this case due to its lesser legal rank, e.g. in comparison to the will. The court held that the declared wish of the deceased should be respected, even if this was not in conformity with the family's religious convictions and beliefs. (Rechtbank Rotterdam, 16 February 2007, ECLI:NL:RBROT:2007:AZ8839)[5]

6.2 Cemeteries

Two kinds of cemeteries are distinguished in the WOL—the municipal and special (*bijzondere begraafplaatsen*), as set out in Art. 24. The 'special' category

5 Available at http://uitspraken.rechtspraak.nl/inziendocument?id=ECLI:NL:RBROT:2007:AZ8839 [last accessed on 9 February 2014].

refers to those cemeteries held by religious communities, as well as by legal and natural persons (Art. 37.1 and Art. 37.2). The prerequisites for the establishment of a cemetery by a religious community are regulated by local authorities (Art. 38). Where a particular community does not have a cemetery at its disposal, municipal authorities will provide it, on request, with an allocated part of a municipal cemetery (Art. 39.1). According to Art. 39.2, municipal authorities are responsible for the management, maintenance and administration of a cemetery, while issues concerning the (e.g. religious) profile, partition and use of allocated parts require consultation with the respective religious community's authorities.

The law does not explicitly regulate the conditions of the establishment of Islamic cemeteries or delimited areas of municipal cemeteries. Practical issues regarding burials at general municipal cemeteries come within the scope of a municipality's responsibilities and competences.[6] Regarding all the issues concerning the disposition of special cemeteries, the permission of the Mayor and the executive of a municipality is required. However, in Art. 41 of the WOL, it is clearly implied that such permission is to be granted providing there is no infringement of the relevant legal regulations. According to Art. 31.2, the grave may be re-used ten years after the burial. However, as stipulated in Art. 28.1, Dutch law envisages the legal right to extend this period for an 'unlimited period of time'.[7]

Wet op de Lijkbezorging, 7 March 1991

Artikel 24
De begraafplaatsen worden onderscheiden in gemeentelijke en bijzondere.
[...]

6 The competences of a municipality are broadly defined in the Gemeentewet, available at http://wetten.overheid.nl/BWBR0005416 [last accessed on 2 June 2014].

7 The Dutch law regarding the opportunity to re-use graves has evoked Muslims' concerns, in spite of the legal guarantees set out in Art. 28.1. This grievance in some Islamic communities, together with the Islamic practice of directing the body towards Mecca (which cannot always be guaranteed at Dutch cemeteries) may explain why some Muslims are buried in their respective countries. However, other motivational factors should be considered, e.g. the wish to be buried in the country of origin. Due to the high costs of transport, insurance agencies are a popular solution. See the advice of the Council of Social Development (Raad van Maatschappelijke Ontwikkeling): *Etniciteit, binding en burgerschap*, 2001, p. 29. Available at www.adviesorgaan-rmo.nl/ [last visit on 22 December 2013] and Venhorst, Claudia, *Muslim Ritualising. Death in the Netherlands: Death Rites in a Small Town Context* (Berlin: Lit Verlag 2013), p. 44.

Artikel 28

1. Een uitsluitend recht op een graf, welke vorm aan dit recht ook wordt gegeven, kan uitsluitend schriftelijk worden gevestigd. Het recht kan voor onbepaalde tijd of voor een bepaalde tijd van ten minste tien jaar worden verleend. Het voor bepaalde tijd verleende recht wordt op verzoek, mits gedaan binnen twee jaar voor het verstrijken van de termijn, telkens verlengd, met dien verstande dat de houder van de begraafplaats kan bepalen dat een periode van verlenging niet korter is dan vijf jaar en niet langer is dan twintig jaar. Het uitsluitend recht op een graf is geen registergoed.

2. Binnen een jaar na de aanvang van de termijn waarin verlenging van het recht kan worden verzocht doet de houder van de begraafplaats aan de rechthebbende wiens adres hem bekend is, schriftelijk mededeling van het verstrijken van de termijn en van het bepaalde in het eerste lid.

3. Indien niet binnen drie maanden na verzending van de mededeling, bedoeld in het tweede lid, om verlenging van het recht is verzocht, maakt de houder van de begraafplaats de mededeling bekend bij het graf en bij de ingang van de begraafplaats, tot het einde van de periode waarvoor het recht was gevestigd.

4. In geval van kennelijke verwaarlozing van het onderhoud van een particulier graf, kan de houder van de begraafplaats, voor zover de plicht tot onderhoud niet bij hem ligt, deze verwaarlozing vastleggen in een schriftelijke verklaring, die hij toezendt aan de rechthebbende, die binnen één jaar na ontvangst in het onderhoud voorziet.

5. Indien de ontvangst van de verklaring, bedoeld in het vierde lid, niet bevestigd wordt, maakt de houder van de begraafplaats de verklaring bekend bij het graf en bij de ingang van de begraafplaats, gedurende een periode van vijf jaar dan wel totdat in die periode in het onderhoud is voorzien.

6. Indien toepassing is gegeven aan het vierde of vijfde lid en niet alsnog in het onderhoud van het graf is voorzien, vervalt het recht op het graf op het moment dat de periode van één dan wel vijf jaar, bedoeld in het vierde respectievelijk vijfde lid, is verstreken.

7. Indien het recht op het graf nog geen tien jaar is gevestigd op het moment dat de periode, bedoeld in het vijfde lid is verstreken, blijft de bekendmaking in stand totdat de periode van tien jaar is verstreken dan wel totdat in die periode in het onderhoud is voorzien. Indien niet voordien in het onderhoud van het graf is voorzien, vervalt het recht op het graf zodra de termijn van tien jaar is verstreken.

Artikel 29
1. Een lijk wordt slechts opgegraven met vergunning van de burgemeester van de gemeente waarin het is begraven, en, indien het een particulier graf betreft, met toestemming van de rechthebbende op het graf.
2. Aan de vergunning verbindt de burgemeester de nodige voorschriften betreffende geneeskundig toezicht alsmede vervoer en bestemming van het lijk.
3. Een opgegraven lijk mag worden gecremeerd, wanneer het verzoek daartoe gedaan wordt door de in artikel 18 bedoelde persoon. De paragrafen 1, 2 en 3 van hoofdstuk II zijn ten aanzien van de crematie niet van toepassing.
4. Crematie binnen een jaar na de begraving vindt slechts plaats met schriftelijk verlof van de officier van justitie van de plaats van opgraving.

Artikel 30
Artikel 29 is niet van toepassing bij een opgraving ingevolge een bevel van een gerechtelijke autoriteit met het oog op een strafrechtelijk onderzoek.

Artikel 31
1. Artikel 29 geldt evenmin bij het ruimen van graven, voorzover dit geschiedt met inachtneming van het bepaalde bij of krachtens dit artikel.
2. Het ruimen geschiedt niet dan op last van de houder van de begraafplaats en na verloop van tien jaar nadat in het graf laatstelijk een lijk is geplaatst, en, indien het een particulier graf betreft, met toestemming van de rechthebbende op het graf.
3. De overblijfselen der lijken worden op een begraafplaats ter aarde besteld of, met overeenkomstige toepassing van het gestelde in artikel 29, derde lid, in een crematorium gecremeerd.
4. Gedeputeerde staten kunnen besluiten de in het tweede lid genoemde termijn te verlengen. Het besluit treedt terstond in werking.
5. Ten minste twee maanden voordat een graf van een onbekende wordt geruimd, geeft de houder de burgemeester daarvan kennis. De burgemeester is bevoegd, uitsluitend ten behoeve van de identificatie van de onbekende en opsporing van vermiste personen, van de overblijfselen van de onbekende door of onder verantwoordelijkheid van een arts lichaamsmateriaal af te doen nemen of een gebitsstatus te doen opmaken. Indien de burgemeester van die bevoegdheid gebruik maakt, wordt de ruiming opgeschort, ten minste tot het moment dat de uitslag van de poging tot identificatie bekend is, waarna een nabestaande in de lijkbezorging voorziet dan wel de ruiming kan worden voltooid.

Artikel 32
Bij algemene maatregel van bestuur kunnen regels worden gesteld omtrent de wijze van begraven, de inrichting van het graf, de afstand van de graven onderling, het ruimen van de graven, het verwijderen van grafmonumenten en de teraardebestelling van de overblijfselen der lijken.
[...]

Artikel 37
1. Een bijzondere begraafplaats kan slechts worden aangelegd en in stand gehouden door een kerkgenootschap dan wel door een privaatrechtelijke rechtspersoon of een natuurlijk persoon.
2. Onder kerkgenootschap wordt mede verstaan een onderdeel daarvan of een rechtspersoon, in het leven geroepen door een of meer kerkgenootschappen of onderdelen daarvan.

Artikel 38
Een kerkgenootschap is gerechtigd tot het hebben van één of meer kerkelijke begraafplaatsen tot een zodanige uitgestrektheid, als overeenkomt met een redelijk deel van de grond, welke in de gemeente voor begraafplaatsen bestemd is. De gemeenteraad kan aan een kerkgenootschap op zijn verzoek toestaan, meer of grotere begraafplaatsen te hebben, onverminderd het recht van de andere kerkgenootschappen, bedoeld in de eerste volzin.

Artikel 39
1. Voor zover een kerkgenootschap geen gebruik maakt van de bevoegdheid, bedoeld in artikel 38 wordt op zijn verzoek door burgemeester en wethouders een deel van de gemeentelijke begraafplaats te zijner beschikking gesteld.
2. De gemeente blijft belast met het beheer, het onderhoud en de administratie. Over de inrichting, de afscheiding en het gebruik van genoemd deel der begraafplaats, alsmede over de toepassing van de artikelen 35, 43 en 44, wordt overleg gepleegd met het kerkgenootschap.
[...]

Artikel 41
Voor het in gebruik nemen van de bijzondere begraafplaats of van een deel daarvan is de toestemming van burgemeester en wethouders nodig. Deze toestemming wordt slechts geweigerd, indien niet aan de wettelijke voorschriften is voldaan.

CHAPTER 7

Education and Schools

The Dutch system of education has been broadly debated in the Netherlands since the 19th century, triggering 'school battles', constitutional amendments and wide-ranging debates on the national and cultural identity of Dutch society. It is worth noting that the Dutch system is to a certain extent unique by providing the legal foundations for the state funding of schools regardless of their (worldview or religious) profile. This system, formally established at the beginning of the 20th century, has evoked a range of controversies and questions concerning the principle of the separation of church and state, as well as the shape of Dutch society, primarily with respect to the post-war processes of pluralisation. One of the broadly discussed and analysed matters was the conformity of the Dutch concept of education (particularly state funding of faith-based schools, and the organisation of religious instructions in public schools at the expense of the taxpayer) with the Dutch Constitution.

7.1 Compulsory Education

The fundamental legal act regarding the Dutch system of education is the Dutch Constitution, whose Art. 23 explicitly refers to this issue. Art. 23 is derived in an almost unchanged form from the constitutional statement of 1917 (the Pacification of 1917)[1] and has a long tradition in the history of Dutch legislation. One should note that, historically, the issue of education played a crucial role in the development of the pillar-based society in the Netherlands.

Dutch law does not explicitly refer to Islamic schools or Islamic religious education at public schools. However, general conditions and rules in this regard may be interpreted from the legislation. According to the Constitution, the state is responsible for the system of education, i.e. both its quality and organisation (Art. 23.1). According to Dutch law, the system of public education

1 Leenknegt, Gert-Jan, *Vrijheid van onderwijs in vijf Europese landen. Een rechtswergelijkend onderzoek naar de gemeenschappelijke rechtsbeginselen op het gebied van het onderwijs in België, Duitsland, Engeland, Frankrijk en Nederland* (Tilburg: Uitgeverij van het Schoordijk Instituut, 1997), p. 133.

should be based on the principle of respect for one's religion or worldview, as further stipulated in Art. 23.3. As stipulated in Art. 23.4, a municipality is responsible for providing a sufficient number of schools and guaranteeing access to education. The Constitution also guarantees state funding of the system of education (Art. 23.5, Art. 23.6, Art. 23.7).

Dutch law distinguishes two general types of schools, i.e. public schools (*openbare scholen*, i.e. 'state schools') and 'special' schools (*bijzondere scholen*, i.e. schools based on certain religious or worldview principles, organised and managed by school boards). The shape and conditions of the Dutch system of education are set out in the Act on Primary Education (Wet op het primair onderwijs, hereafter WPO), as amended, and the Act on Secondary Education (Wet op het voortgezet onderwijs, hereafter WVO), as amended. With regard to compulsory education, both acts state that the process of education and development of pupils should involve special attention being given to 'religious, worldview and social values', and a non-discrimination policy based on respect for a pupil's religious or worldview convictions (Art. 46 of the WPO; Art. 42 of the WVO).

Grondwet voor het Koninkrijk der Nederlanden

Artikel 23

1. Het onderwijs is een voorwerp van de aanhoudende zorg der regering.
2. Het geven van onderwijs is vrij, behoudens het toezicht van de overheid en, voor wat bij de wet aangewezen vormen van onderwijs betreft, het onderzoek naar de bekwaamheid en de zedelijkheid van hen die onderwijs geven, een en ander bij de wet te regelen.
3. Het openbaar onderwijs wordt, met eerbiediging van ieders godsdienst of levensovertuiging, bij de wet geregeld.
4. In elke gemeente wordt van overheidswege voldoend openbaar algemeen vormend lager onderwijs gegeven in een genoegzaam aantal openbare scholen. Volgens bij de wet te stellen regels kan afwijking van deze bepaling worden toegelaten, mits tot het ontvangen van zodanig onderwijs gelegenheid wordt gegeven, al dan niet in een openbare school.
5. De eisen van deugdelijkheid, aan het geheel of ten dele uit de openbare kas te bekostigen onderwijs te stellen, worden bij de wet geregeld, met inachtneming, voor zover het bijzonder onderwijs betreft, van de vrijheid van richting.
6. Deze eisen worden voor het algemeen vormend lager onderwijs zodanig geregeld, dat de deugdelijkheid van het geheel uit de openbare kas bekostigd bijzonder onderwijs en van het openbaar onderwijs even afdoende wordt

gewaarborgd. Bij die regeling wordt met name de vrijheid van het bijzonder onderwijs betreffende de keuze der leermiddelen en de aanstelling der onderwijzers geëerbiedigd.
7. Het bijzonder algemeen vormend lager onderwijs, dat aan de bij de wet te stellen voorwaarden voldoet, wordt naar dezelfde maatstaf als het openbaar onderwijs uit de openbare kas bekostigd. De wet stelt de voorwaarden vast, waarop voor het bijzonder algemeen vormend middelbaar en voorbereidend hoger onderwijs bijdragen uit de openbare kas worden verleend.
8. De regering doet jaarlijks van de staat van het onderwijs verslag aan de Staten-Generaal.

Wet op het primair onderwijs, 2 July 1981[2]

Artikel 46. Karakter openbaar onderwijs
1. Het openbaar onderwijs draagt bij aan de ontwikkeling van de leerlingen met aandacht voor de godsdienstige, levensbeschouwelijke en maatschappelijke waarden zoals die leven in de Nederlandse samenleving en met onderkenning van de betekenis van de verscheidenheid van die waarden.
2. Openbare scholen zijn toegankelijk voor alle kinderen zonder onderscheid van godsdienst of levensbeschouwing.
3. Openbaar onderwijs wordt gegeven met eerbiediging van ieders godsdienst of levensbeschouwing.
[...]

Artikel 58. Geen weigering toelating op grond van godsdienstige gezindheid of levensbeschouwing
1. Indien binnen redelijke afstand van de woning van de leerling geen gelegenheid bestaat tot het volgen van openbaar onderwijs, mag de toelating tot de school niet worden geweigerd op grond van godsdienstige gezindheid of levensbeschouwing. Het voorgaande is niet van toepassing indien de school uitsluitend is bestemd voor interne leerlingen.
2. Leerlingen die ingevolge het eerste lid zijn toegelaten, kunnen niet worden verplicht godsdienstonderwijs of levensbeschouwelijk vormingsonderwijs te volgen.

2 Wet op het primair onderwijs, available at http://wetten.overheid.nl/BWBR0003420 [last accessed on 2 June 2014].

Wet op het voortgezet onderwijs, 14 February 1963[3]

Artikel 42. Karakter openbaar onderwijs
1. Het openbaar onderwijs draagt bij aan de ontwikkeling van de leerlingen met aandacht voor de godsdienstige, levensbeschouwelijke en maatschappelijke waarden zoals die leven in de Nederlandse samenleving, en met onderkenning van de betekenis van de verscheidenheid van die waarden.
2. Openbare scholen zijn toegankelijk voor leerlingen zonder onderscheid naar godsdienst of levensbeschouwing.
3. Openbaar onderwijs wordt gegeven met eerbiediging van ieders godsdienst of levensbeschouwing.
[...]

Artikel 44
1. Het onderwijs aan openbare scholen wordt gegeven met eerbiediging van ieders geloofs- of levensovertuiging.
2. Wij kunnen hem, die zich in dit opzicht aan plichtsverzuim schuldig maakt, voor ten hoogste een jaar en bij herhaling voor onbepaalde tijd in zijn bevoegdheid tot het geven van onderwijs aan een openbare school schorsen.

Leerplichtwet 1969[4]

§ 2. Leerplicht
Artikel 2. Verantwoordelijke personen
1. Degene die het gezag over een jongere uitoefent, en degene die zich met de feitelijke verzorging van een jongere heeft belast, zijn verplicht overeenkomstig de bepalingen van deze wet te zorgen, dat de jongere als leerling van een school staat ingeschreven en deze school na inschrijving geregeld bezoekt. Bij de inschrijving wordt een van overheidswege verstrekt document of een bewijs van uitschrijving van een andere school overgelegd waarop de gegevens van de jongere betreffende zijn geslachtsnaam, voorletters, geboortedatum, geslacht en burgerservicenummer of bij gebreke daarvan zo mogelijk zijn onderwijsnummer zijn vermeld. Indien de in de eerste volzin bedoelde

3 Wet op het voortgezet onderwijs, available at http://wetten.overheid.nl/BWBR0002399 [last accessed on 2 June 2014].

4 Leerplichtwet 1969, available at http://wetten.overheid.nl/BWBR0002628 [last accessed on 2 June 2014].

personen bij de inschrijving aannemelijk hebben gemaakt dat zij geen burgerservicenummer of onderwijsnummer van de jongere kunnen overleggen, leggen zij het burgerservicenummer of onderwijsnummer van de jongere over aan de school zodra zij daarvan kennis hebben verkregen.
[...]

§ 3. Vrijstellingen
Artikel 5. Gronden voor vrijstelling van inschrijving
De in artikel 2, eerste lid, bedoelde personen zijn vrijgesteld van de verplichting om te zorgen, dat een jongere als leerling van een school onderscheidenlijk een instelling staat ingeschreven, zolang
a. de jongere op lichamelijke of psychische gronden niet geschikt is om tot een school onderscheidenlijk een instelling te worden toegelaten;
b. zij tegen de richting van het onderwijs op alle binnen redelijke afstand van de woning—of, indien zij geen vaste verblijfplaats hebben, op alle binnen Nederland—gelegen scholen onderscheidenlijk instellingen waarop de jongere geplaatst zou kunnen worden, overwegende bedenkingen hebben;
c. de jongere als leerling van een inrichting van onderwijs buiten Nederland staat ingeschreven en deze inrichting geregeld bezoekt.

Artikel 6. Kennisgeving vrijstelling leerplicht
1. De in artikel 2, eerste lid, bedoelde personen kunnen zich slechts beroepen op vrijstelling, indien zij aan burgemeester en wethouders van de gemeente waar de jongere als ingezetene met een adres in de basisregistratie personen is ingeschreven, hebben kennis gegeven van:
a. de gegevens van de jongere betreffende:
1°. het persoonsgebonden nummer;
2°. de naam, de geboortedatum, het geslacht, het adres en de woonplaats, de postcode van de woonplaats; en
3°. of eerder een beroep op vrijstelling van de leerplicht is gedaan.
b. op welke grond zij een beroep op vrijstelling menen te mogen maken.
2. Deze kennisgeving moet worden ingediend:
a. ten minste een maand voordat de jongere leerplichtig wordt, indien zij betrekking heeft op de aanvang van de leerplicht, en
b. zolang nadien aanspraak op vrijstelling wordt gemaakt, elk jaar opnieuw voor 1 juli.
[...]
4. Burgemeester en wethouders verstrekken aan Onze Minister de volgende gegevens van de jongere voor wie op grond van het eerste lid een beroep op vrijstelling wordt gedaan:

a. het persoonsgebonden nummer, de postcode van de woonplaats;
b. de begin- en einddatum van de vrijstelling;
c. of eerder beroep is gedaan op de vrijstelling van de leerplicht; en
d. indien de jongere niet eerder onderwijs binnen Nederland heeft gevolgd: de naam, adres en woonplaats, geslacht en geboortedatum.
5. Onze Minister neemt de volgende op grond van het vierde lid door burgemeester en wethouders verstrekte gegevens op in het register vrijstellingen en vervangende leerplicht:
a. het persoonsgebonden nummer;
b. de begin- en einddatum van de vrijstelling;
c. of eerder een beroep op vrijstelling van de leerplicht is gedaan;
d. de woongemeente; en
e. het gegeven dat het een vrijstelling van de leerplicht betreft.
[...]

Artikel 8. Bedenkingen tegen richting van school
1. Een beroep op vrijstelling op grond van artikel 5 onder b kan slechts worden gedaan, indien de kennisgeving de verklaring bevat, dat tegen de richting van het onderwijs op alle binnen redelijke afstand van de woning—of, bij het ontbreken van een vaste verblijfplaats, op alle binnen Nederland—gelegen scholen onderscheidenlijk instellingen waarop de jongere geplaatst zou kunnen worden, overwegende bedenkingen bestaan.
2. Deze verklaring is niet geldig, indien de jongere in het jaar, voorafgaande aan de dagtekening van de kennisgeving, geplaatst is geweest op een school onderscheidenlijk een instelling van de richting waartegen bedenkingen worden geuit.
[...]

Artikel 11. Gronden voor vrijstelling van geregeld schoolbezoek
De in artikel 2, eerste lid, bedoelde personen zijn vrijgesteld van de verplichting te zorgen dat de jongere de school waarop hij staat ingeschreven, geregeld bezoekt, en de leerplichtige jongere die de leeftijd van 12 jaren heeft bereikt alsmede de jongere die kwalificatieplichtig is, zijn vrijgesteld van de verplichting de school of de instelling geregeld te bezoeken, indien
[...]
e. de jongere wegens vervulling van plichten voortvloeiend uit godsdienst of levensovertuiging verhinderd is de school onderscheidenlijk de instelling te bezoeken;

Jurisprudence

Case 1

The court held that the respondent did not have the legal right to refuse to enrol his daughter in a school. The respondent based his argument on his religious (Islamic) convictions and referred to the Leerplichtwet 1969, which envisages the opportunity for such a refusal. According to the respondent, the schools available in their catchment area did not have an Islamic profile, which was the main argument in the declaration he submitted to the municipal authorities, in accordance with the respective legal provisions. The court held that the argument did not include sufficient well-founded objections addressed to the profile of education offered by the schools in the respondent's catchment area. It was thereby decided that the respondent would be obliged to enrol his daughter in a school. (Rb. Amsterdam 13 December 2011, no. 13/883.081-11[5]) However, the respondent had the charges against him withdrawn by the Court of Appeal. (Gerechtshof Amsterdam, 5 April 2012, ECLI:NL:GHAMS:2012:BW8249)[6]

7.2 Religious Education

The Dutch legislator has envisaged legal means to organise religious education at public schools. According to Art. 57 of the WPO, the number of hours of religious instruction (or other forms of instructions of a worldview character) may not exceed 120 a year. Such classes may be led by teachers either employed by the school or affiliated to external entities. This form of religious education exists both at primary and secondary levels. Schools are obliged to organise other lessons for pupils who do not attend such classes during this time.

In 2006 the Dutch Inspectorate of Education analysed the legal situation of public education in the Netherlands at the request of the Ministry of Education, Culture and Science. The Inspectorate deemed that organising religious education at public schools did not contravene the Constitution or the principle of the separation of church and state. Moreover, state funding of such lessons was assumed to be acceptable within the boundaries of the existing law. However, further standardisation of this system was advised.[7]

---

5 Available at http://uitspraken.rechtspraak.nl/inziendocument?id=ECLI:NL:RBAMS:2011:BU8410 [last accessed on 10 February 2014].

6 Available at http://uitspraken.rechtspraak.nl/inziendocument?id=ECLI:NL:GHAMS:2012:BW8249 [last accessed on 10 February 2014].

7 See *Dienstverband, godsdienst en de openbare school. Over de aanstelling van de leraren godsdienst en levensbeschouwelijke vorming op de openbare school,* Onderwijsraad 2006, no.

In December 2008 the Dutch Parliament introduced an amendment to budget law on the basis of which the state took over the duty of financing religious and humanistic education in public schools.[8] Such lessons are organised at the parents' request, usually in the form of one hour's tuition per week. The money is paid to the organisations and religious communities to which the teachers of religion or humanism are affiliated. On the basis of this regulation, all schools, regardless of their worldview orientation, have equal access to state subsidies providing the required criteria are met.[9]

Wet op het primair onderwijs

Artikel 50. Mogelijkheid godsdienstonderwijs of levensbeschouwelijk vormingsonderwijs
Het bevoegd gezag stelt de leerlingen in de gelegenheid op de school, binnen de schooltijden, godsdienstonderwijs of levensbeschouwelijk vormingsonderwijs te ontvangen. Van de tijd daaraan te besteden worden ten hoogste 120 uren per schooljaar meegeteld voor het aantal uren onderwijs dat de leerlingen krachtens artikel 8, zevende lid, aanhef en onder b, ten minste moeten ontvangen. Voor de leerlingen die dit onderwijs niet volgen, voorziet het bevoegd gezag in andere onderwijsactiviteiten op de school.

Artikel 51. Leraren godsdienstonderwijs of levensbeschouwelijk vormingsonderwijs
Godsdienstonderwijs wordt gegeven door leraren daartoe aangewezen door kerkelijke gemeenten, plaatselijke kerken, of rechtspersonen met volledige rechtsbevoegdheid die zich blijkens hun statuten het geven van godsdienstonderwijs ten doel stellen. Levensbeschouwelijk vormingsonderwijs wordt

20060113/859, available at http://www.onderwijsraad.nl/upload/documents/publicaties/volledig/dienstverband_godsdienst_en_de_openbare_school.pdf. [last accessed on 10 January 2014].

8 *Vaststelling van de begrotingsstaten van het Ministerie van Onderwijs, Cultuur en Wetenschap (VIII) voor het jaar 2009* (31700 VIII, No. 79), available at http://www.europa-nu.nl/9353000/1/j4nvgs5kjg27kof_j9vvikqpopjt8zm/vios9doxyyzp/f=/kst125607.pdf [last accessed on 2 June 2014].

9 See e.g. Vries, Jurn P. de (Chairman of Association for Religious and Humanist Education—Stichting Dienstencentrum GVO en HVO), *Wat is het godsdienstig en levensbeschouwelijk vormingsonderwijs (GVO en HVO) op de openbare basisschool?*, 2010, p. 2, available at http://www.gvoenhvo.nl/pers-en-publicaties/pers-downloads/wat-is-het-g-hvo-juni-2010.pdf [last accessed on 2 June 2014].

gegeven door leraren daartoe aangewezen door volledige rechtsbevoegdheid bezittende organisaties op geestelijke grondslag.
Het bevoegd gezag ziet erop toe dat dit onderwijs uitsluitend wordt gegeven door een leraar die blijkens een daartoe strekkende verklaring van de aanwijzende instantie:
a. voldoet aan de bekwaamheidseisen die krachtens artikel 32a, eerste lid, voor het geven van dat onderwijs zijn vastgesteld, en
b. zijn bekwaamheid onderhoudt.
[...]

Artikel 57. Godsdienstonderwijs of levensbeschouwelijk vormingsonderwijs
Onverminderd artikel 9 kunnen de onderwijsactiviteiten godsdienstonderwijs of levensbeschouwelijk vormingsonderwijs omvatten. Van de tijd daaraan te besteden worden ten hoogste 120 uren per schooljaar meegeteld voor het aantal uren onderwijs dat de leerlingen krachtens artikel 8, zevende lid, aanhef en onder b, ten minste moeten ontvangen. Het geven van godsdienstonderwijs of levensbeschouwelijk vormingsonderwijs kan worden opgedragen aan een niet aan de school verbonden leraar.

Wet op het voortgezet onderwijs

Artikel 46
1. Aan de openbare scholen worden op verzoek van kerkelijke gemeenten of van plaatselijke kerken de leerlingen in de gelegenheid gesteld in de schoollokalen godsdienstonderwijs te volgen van godsdienstleraren, daartoe door die gemeenten of kerken aan te wijzen.
2. De schoollokalen worden, zo nodig verwarmd en verlicht, kosteloos voor het godsdienstonderwijs beschikbaar gesteld.
3. Bij een geschil omtrent het vaststellen van lessen of het beschikbaar stellen van lokalen van openbare scholen beslist Onze minister.
4. Aan de kerkelijke gemeenten of de plaatselijke kerken kan een subsidie worden verstrekt. De artikelen 4 tot en met 19 van de Wet overige OCW-subsidies zijn van toepassing, met dien verstande dat de subsidie slechts kan worden verstrekt bij algemene maatregel van bestuur.
5. Voor de toepassing van dit artikel worden met kerkelijke gemeenten gelijkgesteld verenigingen met volledige rechtsbevoegdheid, die zich blijkens de statuten het geven of doen geven van godsdienstonderwijs ten doel stellen.
6. Het bevoegd gezag ziet erop toe dat dit onderwijs uitsluitend wordt gegeven door een leraar die blijkens een daartoe strekkende verklaring van de aanwijzende kerkelijke gemeente of plaatselijke kerk:

a. voldoet aan de bekwaamheidseisen die krachtens artikel 36, eerste lid, voor het geven van dat onderwijs zijn vastgesteld, en
b. zijn bekwaamheid onderhoudt.

Artikel 47
1. Aan de openbare scholen worden op verzoek van door Ons tot dit doel toegelaten genootschappen op geestelijke grondslag de leerlingen, wier ouders, voogden of verzorgers daartoe de wens te kennen geven, in de gelegenheid gesteld in de schoollokalen levensbeschouwelijk vormingsonderwijs te volgen van leraren, daartoe door deze genootschappen aan te wijzen.
2. De schoollokalen worden, zo nodig verwarmd en verlicht, kosteloos voor het vormingsonderwijs beschikbaar gesteld.
3. Bij een geschil omtrent het vaststellen van lessen of het beschikbaar stellen van lokalen van openbare scholen beslist Onze minister.
4. Aan de genootschappen, bedoeld in het eerste lid, kan een subsidie worden verstrekt. De artikelen 4 tot en met 19 van de Wet overige OCW-subsidies zijn van toepassing, met dien verstande dat de subsidie slechts kan worden verstrekt bij algemene maatregel van bestuur.
5. Het bevoegd gezag ziet erop toe dat dit onderwijs uitsluitend wordt gegeven door een leraar die blijkens een daartoe strekkende verklaring van het aanwijzend genootschap op geestelijke grondslag:
a. voldoet aan de bekwaamheidseisen die krachtens artikel 36, eerste lid, voor het geven van dat onderwijs zijn vastgesteld, en
b. zijn bekwaamheid onderhoudt.

7.3 Special Schools

The Dutch constitutional idea of the freedom of education refers to two dimensions. First, it pertains to the right to establish schools (*oprichten*) as stipulated in Art. 23.2, and, second, to the right to define a school's worldview profile (*inrichten*) as stated in Art. 23.5. This also involves a school's relative autonomy regarding the content of the education offered. Art. 23.3 additionally guarantees respect for a pupil's religious or worldview convictions. According to Dutch law, schools are entirely financed by the state providing they fulfil the formal requirements. The state has the right to control the quality of education and teaching staff's qualifications. Inspections are regularly conducted by the relevant entity from the Ministry of Education, Culture and Science, i.e. the Inspectorate of Education (*Onderwijsinspectie*). Moreover, according to Art. 7.1, the WPO does not embrace schools which are aimed solely at the education of pupils of non-Dutch nationality. Aside from 'special' schools financed by the state, one can also distinguish schools which are materially independent of the government. However, in their case particular legal requirements should also be fulfilled.[10]

A special (e.g. religiously-oriented) school has the right to refuse the enrolment of a pupil whose denomination or philosophy of life compromises the religious or ideological grounds of the school.[11] Nevertheless, both the WPO and WVO state that in cases when no public school falls within a pupil's catchment area, a special school is obliged to enrol a pupil regardless of his or her religious convictions (Art. 58.1 and Art. 48.1, respectively). Moreover, in the aforementioned case, pupils who are accepted at religiously-oriented schools are not obliged to attend religious instruction, according to Art. 58.2 of the WPO and Art. 48.2 of the WVO, if that religious instruction does not conform to their worldview or religious convictions.

The emergence of Islamic-inspired schools within the Dutch system of education elicited a broad public debate. Islamic schools, like other confessional schools, are relatively autonomous with regard to internal rules, as well as defining moral issues and their worldview character (within the limits set by law). Hence, they have the right individually to regulate issues such as e.g. the rules regarding the wearing by females of headscarves, the organisation of physical education for girls and boys (either together or separately),[12] and so forth.

---

10 See Art. 5 of the WPO. Regarding the conditions of state funding of primary schools see also Art. 69 of the WPO, and the following articles. Regarding secondary schools, the conditions of the establishment of schools which are not embraced by state funding are set out in Articles 54–59 of the WVO.

11 http://www.rijksoverheid.nl/onderwerpen/vrijheid-van-onderwijs/openbaar-en-bijzonder-onderwijs#anker-bijzondere-scholen [last accessed on 15 February 2014].

12 The report of the Dutch Ministry of Education, Culture and Science, *Islamitische scholen en sociale cohesie*, Utrecht 2002, pp. 9–21, available at http://www.onderwijsinspectie.nl/binaries/content/assets/Actueel_publicaties/2002/Islamitische+scholen+en+sociale+cohesie.pdf [last accessed on 2 June 2014]. See also Meij, Leo van der, *De identiteit van het islamitisch onderwijs in Nederland*, ISBO 2010, p. 6, available at http://www.deisbo.nl/wp-content/uploads/2009/03/identiteitislamitischonderwijs.pdf [last accessed on 30 October 2010] concerning the differences between e.g. Moroccan and Turkish schools. The free afternoon that in most Dutch schools is scheduled on Wednesday is moved to Friday in Islamic schools to allow for traditional Friday prayers—see Shadid, Koningsveld van, *Islam in Nederland en België* ..., p. 255.

Wet op het primair onderwijs

Artikel 5. Niet uit de openbare kas bekostigd bijzonder schoolonderwijs
Het bevoegd gezag van een bijzondere school geeft binnen vier weken na de oprichting van de school onder overlegging van de statuten van de rechtspersoon, die de school in stand houdt, en van de reglementen, van die oprichting kennis aan Onze minister. Indien de statuten of reglementen worden gewijzigd of ingetrokken, wordt eveneens binnen vier weken van de wijziging of van de intrekking van de statuten of reglementen aan Onze minister kennis gegeven.
[...]

Artikel 7. Reikwijdte wet
1. Deze wet is niet van toepassing op scholen die uitsluitend bestemd zijn voor kinderen die niet de Nederlandse nationaliteit hebben.
2. Bij twijfel of op een school het eerste lid van toepassing is, besluit de Kroon, de Raad van State gehoord.
[...]

Artikel 58. Geen weigering toelating op grond van godsdienstige gezindheid of levensbeschouwing
1. Indien binnen redelijke afstand van de woning van de leerling geen gelegenheid bestaat tot het volgen van openbaar onderwijs, mag de toelating tot de school niet worden geweigerd op grond van godsdienstige gezindheid of levensbeschouwing. Het voorgaande is niet van toepassing indien de school uitsluitend is bestemd voor interne leerlingen.
2. Leerlingen die ingevolge het eerste lid zijn toegelaten, kunnen niet worden verplicht godsdienstonderwijs of levensbeschouwelijk vormingsonderwijs te volgen.

Wet op het voortgezet onderwijs

Artikel 48
1. Indien binnen redelijke afstand van de woning van de leerling niet de gelegenheid bestaat tot het volgen van het onderwijs aan een openbare school, mag aan deze leerling de toegang tot een gelijksoortige, uit de openbare kas bekostigde bijzondere school niet worden geweigerd op grond van levensbeschouwing, tenzij de school uitsluitend bestemd is voor interne leerlingen.
2. Indien tot een bijzondere school ingevolge het eerste lid andere leerlingen worden toegelaten dan voor wie de school in verband met de levensbeschou-

wing wordt in stand gehouden, kunnen deze leerlingen niet worden verplicht tot het volgen van de lessen in de vakken of andere programma-onderdelen, die in verband met die levensbeschouwing worden gegeven.
[…]

Afdeling II. Niet uit de openbare kas bekostigd bijzonder schoolonderwijs

Artikel 54
Het bestuur van een bijzondere school voor voortgezet onderwijs geeft binnen vier weken na de oprichting van de school onder overlegging van de statuten der instelling, die de school in stand houdt, en van de reglementen, van die oprichting kennis aan Onze minister. Indien de statuten of reglementen worden gewijzigd of ingetrokken, wordt eveneens binnen vier weken van de wijziging of van de intrekking van de statuten of reglementen aan Onze minister kennis gegeven.

Artikel 55. Bekwaamheids- en zedelijkheidseisen personeel
1. Algemeen voortgezet onderwijs wordt slechts gegeven door wie voldoet aan artikel 33, eerste lid. De artikelen 33, leden 1a tot en met vijf en veertien tot en met zestien, en 33a zijn van overeenkomstige toepassing.
2. Onderwijsondersteunende werkzaamheden als bedoeld in artikel 36, derde lid, worden met betrekking tot het algemeen voortgezet onderwijs slechts verricht door wie voldoet aan artikel 35, eerste lid. Artikel 35, tweede en derde lid, is van overeenkomstige toepassing.
[…]

Artikel 57
De aanwijzing geschiedt op een daartoe tot Onze minister gericht verzoek van het schoolbestuur. Bij het verzoek worden overgelegd:
a. het schoolplan van de school;
b. bewijsstukken dat wordt voldaan aan de bekwaamheidseisen;
c. de statuten en het reglement van de rechtspersoon met volledige rechtsbevoegdheid, die de school in stand houdt.

Artikel 58
1. Het schoolplan van een ingevolge artikel 56 aangewezen school voldoet ten minste aan de voorschriften, gegeven bij of krachtens de artikelen 6g, 10, 10b, 10d, 11a tot en met 11f, 12 tot en met 15, 22 en 24.
2. Bij wijziging van het schoolplan doet het schoolbestuur daarvan onmiddellijk mededeling aan de inspectie.

3. Onze minister kan ten behoeve van de bijzondere inrichting van het onderwijs aan de school toestaan, dat wordt afgeweken van het eerste lid. Onze minister besluit binnen zes maanden na ontvangst van een aanvraag. Indien de beschikking niet binnen zes maanden kan worden gegeven, stelt Onze minister de aanvrager daarvan in kennis en noemt hij daarbij een termijn waarbinnen de beschikking wel tegemoet kan worden gezien.
4. De naam van de school duidt aan, met welke van de uit de openbare kas bekostigde scholen zij overeenkomt.
5. De voorwaarden voor de toelating tot de school zijn ten minste gelijk aan die, vastgesteld krachtens artikel 27, eerste lid, alsmede de leden 1a en 1b.
6. Artikel 23a1 is van overeenkomstige toepassing.
7. Voor een school die is aangewezen op grond van artikel 56 zijn van overeenkomstige toepassing:
a. de artikelen 103b, eerste, tweede, vijfde tot en met achtste, en tiende tot en met twaalfde lid, met dien verstande dat van de gegevens, bedoeld in artikel 103b, tweede lid, uitsluitend worden verstrekt de gegevens, bedoeld in de onderdelen a tot en met g, en i, van dat lid;
b. artikel 103c;
c. artikel 103d, eerste en derde lid, met dien verstande dat artikel 103d, eerste lid, onderdeel a, wordt gelezen als: Onze Minister voor zover deze gegevens noodzakelijk zijn voor de beleidsvoorbereiding;
d. artikel 103f;
e. de artikelen 27b, 28 en 28a; en
f. de artikelen 118g tot en met 118i.
8. Voor een school die is aangewezen op grond van artikel 56 kan bij ministeriële regeling een nadere specificatie worden gegeven van de gegevens, bedoeld in artikel 103b, tweede lid, voor zover dat lid van overeenkomstige toepassing is verklaard in het zevende lid, onderdeel a, en worden bepaald welke van die gegevens niet langer behoeven te worden verstrekt. Bij ministeriële regeling kunnen voorts regels worden gesteld omtrent de tijdstippen en de wijze van verstrekking van die gegevens. Bij ministeriële regeling worden regels gesteld ter uitvoering van artikel 103d, eerste en derde lid, voor zover die leden van overeenkomstige toepassing zijn verklaard in het zevende lid, onderdeel c, in ieder geval omtrent de inhoud en de samenstelling van de gegevens, de wijze waarop de gegevens worden verstrekt, de tijdstippen waarop de gegevens worden verstrekt, en de perioden waarop de gegevens betrekking hebben.

Artikel 59
Onze minister kan de aanwijzing intrekken, indien niet langer wordt voldaan aan de artikelen 56 en 58, met uitzondering van artikel 58, zevende lid, onder-

deel f, of indien van misbruik van de verleende aanwijzing is gebleken. De aanwijzing kan door Onze minister tevens worden ingetrokken indien het schoolbestuur of het personeel van de school in strijd handelt met artikel 5:20 van de Algemene wet bestuursrecht.

Jurisprudence

Case 1

Special (including religiously-oriented) schools have the right autonomously to introduce their own regulations, including rules concerning the dress code. Religiously-oriented schools have the right to introduce a ban on wearing particular outfits, and can require the wearing of e.g. Islamic headscarves. (Rb. Haarlem 4 April 2011, ECLI:NL:RBHAA:2011:BQ0063)[13]

Case 2

The applicants (followers of Judaism) wanted to enrol their child in an orthodox Protestant school, as they had done in the case of their other children. They were refused as they applied for the school's permission for their child to be absent on the Jewish holiday of Passover. The Court held that the school had the right to refuse to agree to the absence, but nevertheless had no right to refuse the enrolment of the child, as the applicants had accepted and signed all the guidelines forming the moral and organisational basis of the school's functioning. The school could report the child's absence to the competent body. In the Court's opinion, the school could not introduce any new regulations after the universal requirements had been fulfilled by the applicants, and decided the child should be enrolled. (Rechtbank Rotterdam, 30 January 2014, ECLI:NL:RBROT:2014:520)[14]

---

13 Available at http://uitspraken.rechtspraak.nl/inziendocument?id=ECLI:NL:RBHAA:2011:BQ0063 [last accessed on 10 February 2014].

14 Available at http://uitspraken.rechtspraak.nl/inziendocument?id=ECLI:NL:RBROT:2014:520 [last accessed on 10 February 2014].

CHAPTER 8

Further and Higher (Tertiary) Education

Since the 1990s, the conditions of the establishment of autonomous academic (Islamic) theological faculties have been broadly discussed in the Netherlands.[1] In January 2002 the Advisory Commission for Imam Training (Adviescommissie Imamopleidingen)[2] was established by the Dutch Minister of Education, Culture and Science. The main task of this committee was to investigate the conditions of both the organisation (including the indication of representative bodies) and funding opportunities for imam training.[3] Nevertheless, there are no detailed legislative provisions (other than general educational legislation) governing the issue.

Owing to the number and internal heterogeneity of Islamic communities in the Netherlands, no one model of imam training can be distinguished, and each Islamic grouping may present its own vision of both the educational background and the perceived role of an imam. Here, one should also note that the Act on Higher Education and Scientific Research (Wet op het Hoger Onderwijs en Wetenschappelijk Onderzoek, hereafter WHW), as amended, distinguishes the category of worldview-oriented universities (*levensbeschouwelijke universiteiten*) (Art. 1.3 § 2).[4]

---

1 See also Shadid, van Koningsveld, *Islam in Nederland en België ...*, pp. 71–78. The first Islamic theological faculty (at the Bachelor level) was established at the VU University Amsterdam (*Vrije Universiteit Amsterdam*) in 2005. See also the parliamentary debate, e.g. the motion no. 143, Tweede Kamer 2003–2004, 29 200 VI, no. 143, available online at http://www.parlementairemonitor.nl/9353000/1/j4nvgs5kjg27kof_j9vvij5epmj1ey0/vi3am8m3lzym/f=/kst76091.pdf [last accessed on 14 January 2014].

2 The so-called de Ruiter Commission (Commissie de Ruiter), named after its leader, Prof. J. de Ruiter. It should be noted that the representatives of Islamic organisations also participated in the Commission's work.

3 In December 2003 the de Ruiter Commission published its final report, *Imams in Nederland? Wie leidt ze op? Rapport van de Adviescommissie Imamopleidingen.* The report explicitly refers to imam training. The position of imams and Islamic chaplains in public institutions has primarily been emphasised.

4 Private (religiously or worldview-oriented) educational institutions, including those for tertiary education, are generally not funded by the state, which is argued by the principle of the separation of church and state. Nevertheless, the Dutch state reveals a certain flexibility in this regard. In each case a range of requirements concerning the organisation

Wet op het Hoger Onderwijs en Wetenschappelijk Onderzoek, 8 October 1992[5]

Artikel 1.3. Instellingen voor hoger onderwijs
1. Universiteiten zijn gericht op het verzorgen van wetenschappelijk onderwijs en het verrichten van wetenschappelijk onderzoek. In elk geval verzorgen zij initiële opleidingen in het wetenschappelijk onderwijs, verrichten zij wetenschappelijk onderzoek, voorzien zij in de opleiding tot wetenschappelijk onderzoeker of technologisch ontwerper en dragen zij kennis over ten behoeve van de maatschappij.
2. Levensbeschouwelijke universiteiten zijn gericht op het verzorgen van wetenschappelijk onderwijs voor een levensbeschouwelijk ambt of beroep. Zij verrichten wetenschappelijk onderzoek op levensbeschouwelijk terrein, voorzien in de opleiding tot wetenschappelijk onderzoeker en dragen kennis over ten behoeve van de maatschappij.
3. Hogescholen zijn gericht op het verzorgen van hoger beroepsonderwijs. Zij verrichten ontwerp- en ontwikkelactiviteiten of onderzoek gericht op de beroepspraktijk. Zij verzorgen in elk geval bacheloropleidingen in het hoger beroepsonderwijs, zij verzorgen in voorkomende gevallen masteropleidingen in het hoger beroepsonderwijs en zij dragen in elk geval kennis over ten behoeve van de maatschappij. Zij dragen bij aan de ontwikkeling van beroepen waarop het onderwijs is gericht.
4. De Open Universiteit is gericht op het verzorgen van wetenschappelijk onderwijs en hoger beroepsonderwijs, het, in overeenstemming met het profiel van de Open Universiteit, verrichten van wetenschappelijk onderzoek en onderzoek gericht op de beroepspraktijk, alsmede het leveren van een bijdrage aan de vernieuwing van het hoger onderwijs. Zij verzorgt in elk geval initiële opleidingen. Zij verzorgt deze in de vorm van afstandsonderwijs.

---

and quality of education need to be fulfilled. The list of the (worldview-oriented) institutions of higher education encompassed by the system of state funding was published in the attachment to the WHW, Bijlage behorende bij de Wet op het hoger onderwijs en wetenschappelijk onderzoek, available at http://wetten.overheid.nl/BWBR0005682/Bijlage [last accessed on 12 January 2014]. However, no Islamic tertiary education institutions are listed.

5 Wet op het Hoger Onderwijs en Wetenschappelijk Onderzoek, available at http://wetten.overheid.nl/BWBR0005682 [last accessed on 12 January 2014].

> 5. De universiteiten, levensbeschouwelijke universiteiten, hogescholen en de Open Universiteit schenken mede aandacht aan de persoonlijke ontplooiing en aan de bevordering van maatschappelijk verantwoordelijkheidsbesef. Zij richten zich in het kader van hun werkzaamheden op het gebied van het onderwijs wat betreft Nederlandstalige studenten mede op de bevordering van de uitdrukkingsvaardigheid in het Nederlands.

8.1 Training of Teachers for Islamic Religious Education

The state sets a range of requirements regarding religious education teachers' qualifications and the quality of education offered. The organisation of religious or humanistic instruction is the duty of a confessional community or other organisational body which represents certain worldviews.[6] All such teachers need to meet the universal requirements, including the proper pedagogical and subject qualifications.[7]

8.2 Islamic Religious Education Training at Universities

Dutch law does not explicitly regulate any issues concerning Islamic education at the higher level and no separate requirements or conditions have been laid down by the law in this regard.

6 See Vries de, *Wat is het godsdienstig en levensbeschouwelijk vormingsonderwijs …*, pp. 1–2.

7 See section 8.2. The general catalogue of the requirements regarding teachers of religion and humanistic education have been included e.g. in the document of the Association for Religious and Humanist Education (*Stichting Dienstencentrum GVO en HVO*), *Competente vakdocenten GVO en HVO voor de openbare basisschool*, Referentiedocument GVO en HVO, Utrecht, 17 May 2010, available at http://www.gvoenhvo.nl/docenten.html [last accessed on 2 June 2014]. The Association is one of the most significant Dutch religious/humanistic education teachers' organisations. All confessional/philosophical communities whose representatives are affiliated to the Association present their own religious curricula. Such programmes are also formed e.g. by the Foundation Platform of Islamic Organisations Rijnmond (Stichting Platform Islamitische Organisaties Rijnmond, SPIOR).

8.3 Imam Training in Public Tertiary Education

Dutch law does not explicitly regulate any issues regarding the organisation and conditions of imam training.[8] However, one should note a special role played by the Dutch-Flemish Accreditation Organisation (Nederlands-Vlaamse Accreditatie Organisatie, hereafter NVAO).[9] The NVAO evaluates tertiary education institutions and is competent to assign accreditations.[10]

8 Regarding the opportunities for imam training see *Integratiebeleid betreffende etnische minderheden in relatie tot hun geestelijke bedienaren*, Tweede Kamer 1997–1998, 25 919, no. 1–2, pp. 25–26, available at https://zoek.officielebekendmakingen.nl/kst-25919-2.html [last accessed on 18 January 2014].

9 The NVAO is defined in Art. 1.1 of the WHW. See Art. 5a § 11 of the WHW regarding the procedures and conditions of accreditation. Among accredited universities offering Islamic studies, one should distinguish those preparing for the position of Islamic education teacher (Hogeschool Inholland in Amsterdam), and chaplains in public institutions and imams (Islamitische Universiteit Rotterdam)—see more at www.nvao.net [last accessed on 14 January 2014].

10 In 2005, two Dutch universities introduced imam training programmes, i.e. the VU University Amsterdam (the Faculty of Theology, Centre for Islamic Theology) and the University of Leiden (the Department of Theology). The training offered was subsidised by the Ministry of Education, Culture and Science. However, in 2011 the Leiden University council decided to remove imam training from the study programme. Heuts, Lars et. al., *Evaluatie Islam- en Imamopleidingen in Nederland*, Eindrapport (Amsterdam: Regioplan Beleidsonderzoek, 2012), pp. 19 and 46–47. Moreover, imam training was introduced at the HBO institution Hogeschool Inholland in Amsterdam. However, in 2013 it was announced that the imam training educational offer at the Inholland Hogeschool would discontinue, *Inholland stopt met imamopleiding*, 8 February 2013, available at http://nos.nl/artikel/471698-inholland-stopt-met-imamopleiding.html [last accessed on 20 January 2014]. In all three cases, state subsidies were assigned. See Heuts, *Evaluatie Islam- en Imamopleidingen …* Besides this, some institutions of tertiary education have introduced Islamic studies (e.g. Christianity and Islam at the University of Tilburg; Islam in the Contemporary World at the University of Utrecht). See Koning de, 'Netherlands', p. 250, and www.nvao.net [last accessed on 18 January 2014]. The establishment of imam training at tertiary education institutions considerably mobilised the CMO and CGI, which engaged in the discussion. Douwes, Koning de, Boender, *Nederlandse moslims …*, p. 91.

8.4 Law on Private Universities

Private universities, i.e. universities which do not benefit from the system of state funding,[11] may apply for an accreditation and be officially recognised by the Ministry of Education, Culture and Science, following a positive evaluation by the NVAO.[12]

---

11 Nevertheless, it should be noted that such universities may apply for ministerial subsidies. See Boender, Welmoet, *Imam in Nederland. Opvattingen over zijn religieuze rol in de samenleving* (Amsterdam: Uitgeverij Bert Bakker, 2007), p. 92, online version available at https://openaccess.leidenuniv.nl/bitstream/handle/1887/12447/Thesis.pdf?sequence=1 [last accessed on 14 January 2014]. As noted by the author, the legislative reasoning in this case finds its origin in the experience of pillarisation.

12 There are two private Islamic universities in the Netherlands, i.e. the Islamic University of Rotterdam (Islamitische Universiteit Rotterdam, hereafter IUR) and the European Islamic University (Islamitische Universiteit van Europa, hereafter IUE) in Schiedam. There are also other institutions providing Islamic education at a higher level. Koning de, 'Netherlands', p. 250. Both the IUR and the IUE were established (in 1997 and 2001, respectively) as independent and autonomous institutions for tertiary education, which are not financially supported by the state and, in turn, have not been taken under the state's control regarding the contents of the education that is offered. See *Imams in Nederland? ...*, p. 10. State recognition involves both the recognition of the grades and certificates obtained, and the opportunity for students to obtain financial support. The IUR was assigned the NVAO accreditation in 2010—the accreditation concerns Islamic chaplaincy training, www.nvao.net [last accessed on 19 January 2014].

CHAPTER 9

Islamic Chaplaincy in Public Institutions

Dutch law regulates the conditions of chaplaincy in public institutions, e.g. the army, prisons, hospitals and care homes.[1] However, there is no single Act which would embody these regulations.[2] The general idea of chaplaincy should be interpreted from Art. 6 of the Dutch Constitution. Other acts regulate the organisation and main conditions of chaplaincy.

Religious services and the presence of religious (including Islamic) chaplains in these institutions are financed by the state.[3] The rules of chaplaincy in penitentiary institutions are regulated by the Prisons Act (Penitentiaire beginselenwet, hereafter PBW), the Act on Care Conditions of the Detained (Beginselenwet verpleging ter beschikking gestelden, hereafter Bvt) and the Regulation on Position-Requirements and Allowance for Chaplains of Other Streams (Regeling functie-eisen en vergoeding geestelijk verzorgers overige stromingen, hereafter Regulation on Chaplains).[4] The conditions of chaplaincy in the army are regulated by the General Military Personnel Regulation (Algemeen militair ambtenarenreglement, hereafter AMAR).

As aforementioned, the conditions of chaplaincy in penitentiary institutions are set out in the Regulation on Chaplains, which refers to 'other' religious tra-

---

1 See Pot, Combertus W. van der, *Handboek van het Nederlandse staatsrecht*, 15th edition (Deventer: Kluwer, 2006), p. 376 and Wal, Peterjan van der, Cuijpers, Mariëlle, *Financiering van geestelijke verzorging voor ouderen. Mogelijkheden voor de verbreding van het werkterrein en de inzet van geestelijk verzorgers*, Vilans/Expertisenetwerk Levensvragen en Ouderen, Utrecht 2012, available at http://www.vilans.nl/docs/producten/fingeestverzorgouderendef.pdf [last accessed on 3 January 2014]. The nominations of candidates are discussed by the government, the CMO and the CGI.

2 Attempts were made in the 1990s to introduce general regulations on chaplaincy issues. The draft was approved by the Tweede Kamer in 1996 but was withdrawn in 1997 by the Eerste Kamer. See *Regels met betrekking tot de geestelijke verzorging in instellingen in de zorgsector, in justitiële inrichtingen en in de krijgsmacht* (*Wet geestelijke verzorging zorginstellingen, justitiële inrichtingen en krijgsmacht*), Eerste Kamer 1995–1996, 23 720, no. 208, available at https://zoek.officielebekendmakingen.nl/kst-19951996-23720-208.html [las accessed on 31 January 2014], see also http://www.eerstekamer.nl/wetsvoorstel/23720_geestelijke_verzorging_zorg [last accessed on 31 January 2014].

3 Regarding the financial links between the state and religious communities, refer to Chapter 3. See more in Pot van der, *Handboek* ..., p. 376.

4 The ministerial regulation (the Ministry of Justice).

ditions, i.e. Islamic, Hindu and Buddhist communities (Art. 1). This regulation pertains to chaplains who are not employed as civil officials. The Regulation on Chaplains regulates the organisation and competences of the Service of Chaplaincy of Judicial Institutions (Dienst Geestelijke Verzorging van de Dienst Justitiële Inrichtingen, hereafter Dienst Geestelijke Verzorging).[5] Moreover, for this function naturalisation is required.

The second group of institutions includes hospitals and care institutions (e.g. homes for the elderly, institutions of social care and so forth). As stipulated in the Act on the Quality of Care Institutions (Kwaliteitswet zorginstellingen), patients and/or residents of health care institutions[6] (i.e. hospitals and other forms of medical institutions, as well as e.g. centres for mental health) are guaranteed access to spiritual counsel (*geestelijke zorg*).[7]

Kwaliteitswet zorginstellingen, 18 January 1996[8]

Artikel 3
De zorgaanbieder organiseert de zorgverlening op zodanige wijze, voorziet de instelling zowel kwalitatief als kwantitatief zodanig van personeel en materieel, en draagt zorg voor een zodanige verantwoordelijkheidstoedeling, dat een en ander leidt of redelijkerwijs moet leiden tot een verantwoorde zorg. Hierbij betrekt hij de resultaten van overleg tussen zorgaanbieders, zorgverzekeraars en patiënten/ consumentenorganisaties. Voor zover het betreft zorgverlening die verblijf van de patiënt of cliënt in de instelling gedurende tenminste het etmaal met zich brengt, draagt de zorgaanbieder er tevens zorg voor dat in de

5 In 2007 the CMO was temporarily recognised by the Ministry and in 2011 it was officially recognised by the Dutch Ministry of Security and Justice as an institution competent to appoint Islamic chaplains in prisons and other detention centres. See Ministerie van Veiligheid en Justitie, *Erkenning Contactorgaan Moslims en Overheid*, Press communiqué, 25 March 2011, available at http://www.rijksoverheid.nl/documenten-en-publicaties/persberichten/2011/03/25/erkenning-contactorgaan-moslims-en-overheid-cmo.html [last accessed on 31 January 2014].

6 Art. 3 refers to the condition requiring a minimum 24-hour stay at such an institution.

7 See also Wet medezeggenschap cliëntenraden zorginstellingen, Art. 3 available at http://wetten.overheid.nl/BWBR0007920 [last accessed on 3 January 2014], Algemene Wet Bijzondere Ziektekosten, available at http://wetten.overheid.nl/BWBR0002614 [last accessed on 3 January 2014], Zorgverzekeringswet, available at http://wetten.overheid.nl/BWBR0018450 [last accessed on 3 January 2014].

8 Kwaliteitswet zorginstellingen, available at http://wetten.overheid.nl/BWBR0007850 [last accessed on 3 January 2014].

instelling geestelijke verzorging beschikbaar is, die zoveel mogelijk aansluit bij de godsdienst of levensovertuiging van de patiënten of cliënten.
[...]

Artikel 5
1. De zorgaanbieder legt jaarlijks vóór 1 juni per instelling een verslag ter openbare inzage, waarin hij verantwoording aflegt van het beleid dat hij in het afgelopen kalenderjaar heeft gevoerd ter uitvoering van de artikelen 2, 3 en 4 en van de kwaliteit van de zorg die hij in dat jaar heeft verleend.
2. In dat verslag geeft de zorgaanbieder daartoe onder meer aan:
a. of en, zo ja, op welke wijze hij patiënten of consumenten bij zijn kwaliteitsbeleid heeft betrokken;
b. de frequentie waarmee en de wijze waarop binnen de instelling kwaliteitsbeoordeling plaatsvond en het resultaat daarvan;
c. welk gevolg hij heeft gegeven aan klachten en meldingen over de kwaliteit van de verleende zorg.
3. Bij ministeriële regeling kunnen nadere regels worden vastgesteld met betrekking tot het verslag.
4. De zorgaanbieder zendt een afschrift van het verslag aan Onze Minister en aan de regionale inspecteur van het staatstoezicht op de volksgezondheid, alsmede aan de organisatie die in de regio de belangen van de patiënten in algemene zin behartigt.

Penitentiaire beginselenwet, 18 June 1998[9]

Artikel 41
1. De gedetineerde heeft het recht zijn godsdienst of levensovertuiging, individueel of in gemeenschap met anderen, vrij te belijden en te beleven.
2. De directeur draagt zorg dat in de inrichting voldoende geestelijke verzorging, die zoveel mogelijk aansluit bij de godsdienst of levensovertuiging van de gedetineerden, beschikbaar is.
3. De directeur stelt de gedetineerde in de gelegenheid op in de huisregels vastgestelde tijden en plaatsen:
a. persoonlijk contact te onderhouden met de geestelijke verzorger van de godsdienst of levensovertuiging van zijn keuze, die aan de inrichting is verbonden;

9 Penitentiaire beginselenwet, available at http://wetten.overheid.nl/BWBR0009709 [last accessed on 2 June 2014].

b. contact te onderhouden met andere dan de onder a genoemde geestelijke verzorgers volgens artikel 38;
c. in de inrichting te houden godsdienstige of levensbeschouwelijke bijeenkomsten van zijn keuze bij te wonen. Artikel 23 is van overeenkomstige toepassing.
4. Bij of krachtens algemene maatregel van bestuur worden nadere regels gesteld ten aanzien van de beschikbaarheid van de geestelijke verzorging. Deze regels hebben betrekking op de verlening van geestelijke verzorging door of vanwege verschillende richtingen van godsdienst of levensovertuiging, op de organisatie en de bekostiging van de geestelijke verzorging en op de aanstelling van geestelijke verzorgers bij een inrichting.

Beginselenwet verpleging ter beschikking gestelden, 25 June 1997[10]

Artikel 40
1. De verpleegde heeft het recht zijn godsdienst of levensovertuiging, individueel of in gemeenschap met anderen, vrij te belijden en te beleven.
2. Het hoofd van de inrichting draagt zorg dat in de inrichting voldoende geestelijke verzorging, die zoveel mogelijk aansluit bij de godsdienst of levensovertuiging van de verpleegden, beschikbaar is.
3. Het hoofd van de inrichting stelt de verpleegde in de gelegenheid op in de huisregels vastgestelde tijden en plaatsen:
a. persoonlijk contact te onderhouden met de geestelijke verzorger van de godsdienst of levensovertuiging van zijn keuze, die aan de inrichting is verbonden;
b. contact te onderhouden met andere dan de onder a genoemde geestelijke verzorgers volgens het bepaalde in artikel 37;
c. in de inrichting te houden godsdienstige en levensbeschouwelijke bijeenkomsten van zijn keuze bij te wonen, tenzij het hoofd van de inrichting dit verbiedt in verband met de handhaving van de orde of de veiligheid in de inrichting.
4. Bij of krachtens algemene maatregel van bestuur kunnen nadere regels worden gesteld ten aanzien van de beschikbaarheid van de geestelijke verzorging. Deze regels kunnen betrekking hebben op de verlening van geestelijke verzorging door of vanwege verschillende richtingen van godsdienst of levensovertuiging, op de organisatie en de bekostiging van de geestelijke verzorging en op de aanstelling van geestelijke verzorgers bij een inrichting.

---

10 Beginselenwet verpleging ter beschikking gestelden, available at http://wetten.overheid.nl/BWBR0008765 [last accessed on 25 January 2014].

Algemeen militair ambtenarenreglement of 25 February 1982[11]

Artikel 1
[...]
5. Voor de toepassing van de hoofdstukken 5, 7, 8, 9 en 10, alsmede de artikelen 39, tweede lid, onderdelen a, f en g, 39a, aanhef en onderdeel e, 44, 49, 126b, 126d tot en met 126f, 130, 134 en 144 tot en met 148, wordt onder "militair" mede begrepen hij die bij het Ministerie van Defensie op grond van artikel 6 van het Burgerlijk ambtenarenreglement defensie is aangesteld in burgerlijke openbare dienst om bij de krijgsmacht als geestelijk verzorger doorlopend werkzaam te zijn. Deze geestelijk verzorger wordt, in voorkomend geval, mede begrepen onder het beroepspersoneel. (...)

Regeling functie-eisen en vergoeding geestelijk verzorgers overige stromingen, 7 June 2002[12]

Artikel 1 Begripsbepalingen
In deze regeling wordt verstaan onder:
a. *geestelijk verzorger*:
een geestelijk verzorger van een overige stroming, te weten: de islamitische, hindoeïstische of boeddhistische gezindte;
b. *justitiabele*:
de gedetineerde, bedoeld in artikel 1, onderdeel e, van de Penitentiaire beginselenwet, de verpleegde, bedoeld in artikel 1, onderdeel j, van de Beginselenwet verpleging ter beschikking gestelden, of de jeugdige, bedoeld in artikel 1, onderdeel f, van de Beginselenwet justitiële jeugdinrichtingen die verblijft in een penitentiaire inrichting onderscheidenlijk een rijksinrichting;
c. *verzoek*:
een verzoek van een justitiabele om geestelijke zorg;

11 Algemeen militair ambtenarenreglement, available at http://wetten.overheid.nl/BWBR0003482 [last accessed on 1 January 2014]. The special position of chaplains in the armed forces is also indicated in the Burgerlijk ambtenarenreglement defensie, available at http://wetten.overheid.nl/BWBR0006040 [last accessed on 1 January 2014]. Moreover, Dutch law designates chaplains as being of equal status to other military officials, see e.g. the Veteranenwet of 11 February 2012, Art. 1b, available at http://wetten.overheid.nl/BWBR0031401 [last accessed on 31 January 2014].

12 Regeling functie-eisen en vergoeding geestelijk verzorgers overige stromingen, available at http://wetten.overheid.nl/BWBR0013751 [last accessed on 31 January 2014].

d. *uurvergoeding*:
een brutobedrag per effectief gewerkt uur;
e. *theologie*:
onder theologie wordt naast westerse christelijke godsdiensten mede verstaan het hindoeïsme, boeddhisme en de islam;
f. *Dienst Geestelijke Verzorging*:
Dienst Geestelijke Verzorging van de Dienst Justitiële Inrichtingen;
g. *portefeuillehouder overige stromingen*:
ambtenaar van de Dienst Geestelijke Verzorging verantwoordelijk voor de organisatie van de geestelijk verzorgers overige stromingen;

Artikel 2 Reikwijdte
Deze regeling is niet van toepassing op de zeer beperkt beveiligde penitentiaire inrichtingen.

Artikel 3 Kwalificaties en functie-eisen geestelijke verzorgers
1. Een geestelijk verzorger kan slechts anders dan bij wijze van ambtelijke aanstelling aan de inrichting worden verbonden indien er een antecedentenonderzoek heeft plaatsgevonden op grond waarvan is vastgesteld dat hiertegen geen bezwaar is. Het antecedentenonderzoek wordt gedaan door het Bureau Integriteit en Veiligheid op verzoek van de portefeuillehouder overige stromingen.
2. Een geestelijk verzorger kan slechts anders dan bij wijze van ambtelijke aanstelling aan de inrichting worden verbonden indien hij:
a. in het bezit is van een geldige verblijfs- en werkvergunning;
b. in het bezit is van een Nederlandse universitaire titel in de theologie dan wel met goed gevolg een afsluitend examen heeft afgelegd op het terrein van de theologie binnen het Nederlands hoger beroepsonderwijs;
c. een verklaring omtrent gedrag overlegt;
d. de Nederlandse taal machtig is in woord; bij twijfel kan de Dienst Geestelijke Verzorging eisen dat een toets in de Nederlandse taal wordt afgelegd;
e. op grond van de Wet inburgering nieuwkomers een inburgeringsprogramma heeft gevolgd.
3. Indien niet aan het gestelde in het tweede lid, onder b, kan worden voldaan, maar er wel een buitenlands diploma op het terrein van de theologie van de desbetreffende gezindte is behaald, vindt er een onderzoek plaats naar de waarde van dit diploma. De geestelijk verzorger kan slechts aan de inrichting worden verbonden indien zijn diploma minimaal op Hbo-niveau wordt gewaardeerd. Deze waardering geschiedt op een door de Dienst Geestelijke Verzorging voorgeschreven wijze.

4. De portefeuillehouder overige stromingen kan van de eis in het derde lid gesteld ontheffing verlenen.
5. Voor de Boeddhistische gezindte kan, indien geen diploma van de desbetreffende gezindte kan worden overgelegd, de geestelijk verzorger worden voorgedragen door de Boeddhistische Unie Nederland als overkoepelend orgaan van zijn gezindte of levensovertuiging.

Artikel 4
Het hoofd van de Dienst Geestelijke Verzorging werft geestelijke verzorgers na overleg met de portefeuillehouder overige stromingen en in samenwerking met de organisaties van de verschillende gezindten. De directeur van de inrichting wordt schriftelijk op de hoogte gesteld van het besluit dat er een kandidaat is gekozen en hoeveel uur hij aan de inrichting wordt verbonden.
[...]

Artikel 6 Uurvergoeding en reiskostenvergoeding
1. De uurvergoeding van de geestelijk verzorger bedraagt een door het hoofd van de Dienst Justitiële Inrichtingen bij besluit vast te stellen bedrag dat verschilt afhankelijk van de opleiding van de geestelijk verzorger.
2. Door de geestelijk verzorgers worden de uurvergoedingen en reiskostenvergoedingen met gebruikmaking van het in de bijlage opgenomen declaratieformulier gedeclareerd bij het Shared Service Center van de Dienst Justitiële Inrichtingen.

Artikel 7 Uitzonderingsbepaling
Deze regeling is niet van toepassing op geestelijk verzorgers met een ambtelijke aanstelling en geestelijk verzorgers die op grond van een mantelovereenkomst met de Dienst Justitiële Inrichtingen werkzaamheden verrichten.

Artikel 8 Registratie geestelijke verzorging
De directeur draagt zorg dat het aantal gevallen waarin een geestelijk verzorger is ingeschakeld alsmede de duur ervan wordt geregistreerd en draagt zorg voor een prestatieverklaring.

CHAPTER 10

Employment and Social Law

Regarding Dutch employment and social law, one should refer to at least three topics, i.e. 1) the regulations concerning the position of ministers of religion (including chaplains), 2) the issue of the protection of religious freedom and non-discrimination policy in employment and social law, and 3) the regulations concerning work relations within religious organisations and the application of Dutch law in this regard. Here, the somewhat 'special' character of religious ministers in the Dutch system of work relations leads to a range of legal perplexities and doubts regarding the character of the relations between an employee and an employer.[1]

10.1 The Principles of Equality and Non-Discrimination in Dutch Employment Law

The non-discrimination principle in Dutch law formed the foundation for the enactment of the Common Equal Treatment Act (*Algemene Wet Gelijke Behandeling*, hereafter AWGB)[2] in 1994. In the same year, on the basis of the AWGB (Articles 11–21), the Equal Treatment Commission (*Commissie Gelijke Behandeling*, hereafter CGB) was created. The main task of the CGB was to scrutinise the claims submitted and investigate the acts of discrimination e.g. on the grounds of ethnicity, gender or religion. Besides this, the CGB had the right to initiate and request surveys and controls. The CGB was an advisory body (its decisions were not binding[3]) and could express its opinions and recommendations with reference to the execution of Dutch law.[4] On 1 October

1 Aerts, Monique C.M., *Sociaal recht. De zelfstandige in het social recht* (Amsterdam: Kluwer 2007), p. 184.

2 See also Chapter 13.

3 Although the opinions, adjudications and recommendations of the CRM are not formally binding, it appears that they are not only followed in practice, but also form a relevant foundation for the legal interpretation of the AWGB's provisions, thereby playing a significant role in Dutch jurisprudence. See e.g. Loenen, *Geloof in het geding* ..., pp. 46–47.

4 See http://cgb.nl/over_de_cgb/oordeelover [last accessed on 20 February 2012]. See also Sauer, Birgit, 'Headscarf regimes in Europe: Diversity Policies at the intersection of gender, culture and religion', *Comparative European Politics*,7 (2009), p. 86.

2012, Articles 11–21 of the AWGB were repealed[5] and the CGB was replaced by the Council for Human Rights (College voor de Rechten van de Mens, hereafter CRM), on the legal basis of the Act on the Council for Human Rights (Wet College voor de Rechten van de Mens, hereafter WCRM),[6] in which the main tasks and competences of the CRM are defined. The CRM expresses its opinions and adjudications in submitted cases, with special emphasis on direct and indirect forms of discrimination.[7]

Ministers of religion (including chaplains) have been assigned a special position in the Dutch system of law and they are not subject to standard forms (contracts) of employment. Traditionally, 'they have ... been regarded as office-holders, not employees'.[8] Regarding the regulations concerning newcomers, one should also refer to the Aliens Employment Act (Wet arbeid vreemdelingen). The position of imams is to a certain extent protected by the system of law, but is at the same time subject to general rules concerning the principles of equality and freedom. The CRM is the competent body to adjudicate on cases of doubt in this regard.[9]

---

5 The amendment of the AWGB of 1 October 2012 was preceded by parliamentary debate, which primarily focused on the definitions of the terms 'direct' and 'indirect' distinction (*direct/indirect onderscheid*). Moreover, it was suggested that the very notion of the 'distinction', which was used in the AWGB, should be replaced by 'discrimination'. These postulations were primarily argued for by the need for Dutch legislation to conform with EU legal standards. See *Wijziging van de Algemene wet gelijke behandeling, het Burgerlijk Wetboek, de Wet gelijke behandeling op grond van handicap of chronische ziekte, de Wet gelijke behandeling op grond van leeftijd bij de arbeid en de Wet gelijke behandeling van mannen en vrouwen* (*aanpassing definities van direct en indirect onderscheid aan richtlijnterminologie*), Tweede Kamer 2010–2011, 31 832, no. 8, available at https://zoek.officielebekendmakingen.nl/kst-31832-8.html [last accessed on 28 January 2014]; Tweede Kamer 2008–2009, 31 832, no. 5, available at http://www.eerstekamer.nl/eu/behandeling/20090302/brief_minister_met_toelichting/f=/vi5qexgyjcs8.pdf [last accessed on 28 January 2014].

6 Wet College voor de Rechten van de Mens, available at http://wetten.overheid.nl/BWBR0030733 [last accessed on 17 January 2014].

7 See also e.g. CGB: 2010-102 concerning the limited flexibility of a Muslim job candidate's working hours due to his religious convictions. The candidate was rejected by a work agency. The CGB did not define this as a form of direct discrimination on religious grounds. Available at https://mensenrechten.nl/publicaties/oordelen/2010-102 [last accessed on 27 January 2014].

8 Doe, Norman, *Law and Religion in Europe. A Comparative Introduction* (New York: Oxford University Press 2011), p. 129. Religious ministers have been e.g. made exempt from the scope of the Extraordinary Order on Work Relations 1945 (Buitengewoon Besluit Arbeidsverhoudingen 1945) of 5 October 1945, as set out in Art. 2c, available at http://wetten.overheid.nl/BWBR0002014 [last accessed on 17 January 2014].

9 See e.g. CGB 2009-129 concerning the penitentiary hospital's rejection of an imam who refused

The general provisions concerning non-discrimination policy (e.g. with reference to one's religious convictions), including in employment law, are set out in Art. 5 of the AWGB. The ban on any form of discrimination concerning one's employment, as well as both work relations and conditions, are explicitly set out in Art. 5.1. In Art. 5.3, the legislator lists cases when religious aspects may be taken into account, thereby forming exceptions from the rule of non-discrimination on the grounds of e.g. religious beliefs, nationality, sexual orientation, gender and so forth, if these aspects form relevant elements of an employing organisation's profile, and when a working relationship is of 'a private character'. Here, one should also refer to the Act on Collective Labour Agreements (Wet op de collectieve arbeidsovereenkomst, hereafter WCA) and the Act on Labour Conditions (Arbeidsomstandighedenwet, hereafter Arbowet). The Arbowet states in Art. 3 that employers should in their policy aim to limit the 'psycho-social burden at work'. This 'burden' also refers to any form of discrimination (including discriminatory acts related to religious convictions).[10] Moreover, the legislator envisages that the dissolution of a labour contract can be recognised as groundless in cases when the performance of the agreed work does not reconcile with an employee's conscience (Art. 681.2e of the BW, Book 7).

Another relevant aspect of Dutch employment law concerns a religious organisation's internal rules and potential autonomy, which play a relevant role in cases when religious profile is essential, e.g. with reference to teachers of religion, or religious organisations' employees. In such cases general labour conditions and rules are usually applied.[11] Nevertheless, as set out in Art. 3 of the AWGB, religious communities and their organisations do not fall within the scope of the AWGB. In this manner the separate position of religious communities has been legally confirmed. It is essential to note that this provision concerns solely the internal affairs of religious communities. In this manner, the principles of equality and non-discrimination have been somewhat 'suspended' with regard to religious communities. This is aimed at allowing them to operate in accordance with their religious rules.[12] Therefore such institutions

---

to shake hands with a female doctor. In the CGB's opinion no direct discrimination occurred. Available at https://mensenrechten.nl/publicaties/oordelen/2009-129 [last accessed on 27 January 2014].

10 See e.g. http://radar.nl/read/juridisch_instrumentarium_bij_discrimina [last accessed on 25 January 2014].

11 Potz, Wieshaider, 'Religious Entities as Legal Persons ...', p. 35.

12 Sap, Jan W., 'Kerk en staat vanuit het staatsrecht. Meer respect voor de publieke dimensie van godsdienst' in *Kerk en recht*, L.C. van Drimmelen, T.J. van der Ploeg (Utrecht: Uit-

may require certain religious affiliation or membership of their employees.[13] Nevertheless, Art. 5.2 of the AWGB explicitly excludes any forms of discrimination (*onderscheid*, literally 'distinction') based on the sole grounds of one's political convictions, race, gender, nationality, sexual orientation or marital status.[14]

The issues concerning the freedom of religion fall within the scope of the CRM's activity. The legal body entitled to adjudicate on cases concerning labour affairs and work conditions is the Central Labour Council (Centrale Raad van Beroep, hereafter CRvB). The role of the CRvB is defined in the Labour Act (Beroepswet).[15]

Algemene Wet Gelijke Behandeling[16]

Artikel 2
1. Het in deze wet neergelegde verbod van onderscheid geldt niet ten aanzien van indirect onderscheid indien dat onderscheid objectief gerechtvaardigd wordt door een legitiem doel en de middelen voor het bereiken van dat doel passend en noodzakelijk zijn.
[...]

geverij LEMMA BV, 2004), p. 107. See also Buitengewoon Besluit Arbeidsverhoudingen 1945 (Art. 2c) of 5 October 1945, available at http://wetten.overheid.nl/BWBR0002014 [last accessed on 3 February 2014].

13 However, as noted e.g. by Pieter S. Fluiten and Wijnand A. Zondag, this provision may cast certain doubts on the character of particular positions within an organisation, as well as the worldview or religious conditions of an individual's employment. In many cases adjudicated on by the CGB (current CRM), the worldview/religious orientation e.g. of a school was considered sufficient justification for the application of strict criteria in this regard. See Fluiten, Pieter S., Zondag, Wijnand A., 'Godsdienst in arbeidsverhoudingen', *Tijdschrift voor arbeid en sociale zekerheid*, SMA 11/12 (2007) (Deventer: Uitg. Kluwer 2007), p. 436. Here one should also note the role of Directive 2000/78/EC.

14 Regarding the political debate preceding the introduction of this provision see Loenen, *Geloof in het geding ...*, pp. 45–46.

15 Beroepswet, available at http://wetten.overheid.nl/BWBR0002170 [last accessed on 28 January 2014].

16 Algemene Wet Gelijke Behandeling, available at http://wetten.overheid.nl/BWBR0006502 [last accessed on 12 June 2014].

Artikel 3
Deze wet is niet van toepassing op:
a. rechtsverhoudingen binnen kerkgenootschappen alsmede hun zelfstandige onderdelen en lichamen waarin zij zijn verenigd, alsmede binnen andere genootschappen op geestelijke grondslag;
b. het geestelijk ambt.
[...]

Artikel 5
1. Onderscheid is verboden bij:
a. de aanbieding van een betrekking en de behandeling bij de vervulling van een openstaande betrekking;
b arbeidsbemiddeling;
c. het aangaan en het beëindigen van een arbeidsverhouding;
d. het aanstellen tot ambtenaar en het beëindigen van het dienstverband van een ambtenaar;
e. arbeidsvoorwaarden;
f. het laten volgen van onderwijs, scholing en vorming tijdens of voorafgaand aan een arbeidsverhouding;
g. bevordering;
h. arbeidsomstandigheden.
2. Het eerste lid laat onverlet:
a. de vrijheid van een instelling op godsdienstige of levensbeschouwelijke grondslag om eisen te stellen, die gelet op het doel van de instelling, nodig zijn voor de vervulling van een functie, waarbij deze eisen niet mogen leiden tot onderscheid op grond van het enkele feit van politieke gezindheid, ras, geslacht, nationaliteit, hetero- of homoseksuele gerichtheid of burgerlijke staat;
b. de vrijheid van een instelling op politieke grondslag om eisen te stellen, die gelet op het doel van de instelling, nodig zijn voor de vervulling van een functie, waarbij deze eisen niet mogen leiden tot onderscheid op grond van het enkele feit van ras, geslacht, nationaliteit, hetero- of homoseksuele gerichtheid of burgerlijke staat en
c. de vrijheid van een instelling van bijzonder onderwijs om eisen te stellen over de vervulling van een functie, die, gelet op het doel van de instelling, nodig zijn voor de verwezenlijking van haar grondslag, waarbij deze eisen niet mogen leiden tot onderscheid op grond van het enkele feit van politieke gezindheid, ras, geslacht, nationaliteit, hetero- of homoseksuele gerichtheid of burgerlijke staat.
3. Het eerste lid is niet van toepassing indien:

a. de werkverhouding een privékarakter heeft,
b. het verschil in behandeling berust op een kenmerk dat verband houdt met godsdienst, levensovertuiging, politieke gezindheid, ras, geslacht, nationaliteit, hetero- of homoseksuele gerichtheid of burgerlijke staat, en
c. dat kenmerk vanwege de aard van de betrokken specifieke beroepsactiviteit of de context waarin deze wordt uitgeoefend, een wezenlijk en bepalend beroepsvereiste vormt, mits het doel legitiem is en het vereiste evenredig is aan dat doel.

Artikel 6a
1. Onderscheid is verboden bij het lidmaatschap van of de betrokkenheid bij een werkgevers- of werknemersorganisatie of een vereniging van beroepsgenoten, alsmede bij de voordelen die uit dat lidmaatschap of uit die betrokkenheid voortvloeien.
2. Het eerste lid laat onverlet:
a. de vrijheid van een op godsdienstige of levensbeschouwelijke grondslag gebaseerde organisatie of vereniging om eisen te stellen, die gelet op haar doel, nodig zijn voor de verwezenlijking van haar grondslag, waarbij deze eisen niet mogen leiden tot onderscheid op grond van het enkele feit van politieke gezindheid, ras, geslacht, nationaliteit, hetero- of homoseksuele gerichtheid of burgerlijke staat en
b. de vrijheid van een op politieke grondslag gebaseerde organisatie of vereniging om eisen te stellen, die gelet op haar doel, nodig zijn voor de verwezenlijking van haar grondslag, waarbij deze eisen niet mogen leiden tot onderscheid op grond van het enkele feit van ras, geslacht, nationaliteit, hetero- of homoseksuele gerichtheid of burgerlijke staat.

Burgerlijk Wetboek Book 7, Bijzondere overeenkomsten[17]

Artikel 681
1. Indien een van de partijen de arbeidsovereenkomst, al of niet met inachtneming van de voor de opzegging geldende bepalingen, kennelijk onredelijk opzegt, kan de rechter steeds aan de wederpartij een schadevergoeding toekennen.
2. Opzegging van de arbeidsovereenkomst door de werkgever zal onder andere kennelijk onredelijk geacht kunnen worden:

17 Burgerlijk Wetboek Book 7, Bijzondere overeenkomsten, available at http://www.wetboek-online.nl/wet/Burgerlijk%20Wetboek%20Boek%207.html#2123 [last accessed on 27 January 2014].

a. wanneer deze geschiedt zonder opgave van redenen of onder opgave van een voorgewende of valse reden;
b. wanneer, mede in aanmerking genomen de voor de werknemer getroffen voorzieningen en de voor hem bestaande mogelijkheden om ander passend werk te vinden, de gevolgen van de opzegging voor hem te ernstig zijn in vergelijking met het belang van de werkgever bij de opzegging;
c. wanneer deze geschiedt in verband met een verhindering van de werknemer om de bedongen arbeid te verrichten als bedoeld in artikel 670 lid 3;
d. wanneer deze geschiedt in afwijking van een in de bedrijfstak of de onderneming krachtens wettige regeling of gebruik geldende getalsverhouding- of anciënniteitsregeling, tenzij hiervoor zwaarwichtige gronden aanwezig zijn;
e. wanneer deze geschiedt wegens het enkele feit dat de werknemer met een beroep op een ernstig gewetensbezwaar weigert de bedongen arbeid te verrichten.
3. Opzegging van de arbeidsovereenkomst door de werknemer zal onder andere kennelijk onredelijk geacht kunnen worden:
a. wanneer deze geschiedt zonder opgave van redenen of onder opgave van een voorgewende of valse reden;
b. wanneer de gevolgen van de opzegging voor de werkgever te ernstig zijn in vergelijking met het belang van de werknemer bij de opzegging.
4. Een beding waarbij aan een van de partijen de beslissing wordt overgelaten of de arbeidsovereenkomst al of niet kennelijk onredelijk is opgezegd, is nietig.

Wet arbeid vreemdelingen, 21 December 1994[18]

Artikel 8
1. Een tewerkstellingsvergunning wordt geweigerd:
a. indien voor de desbetreffende arbeidsplaats prioriteitgenietend aanbod op de arbeidsmarkt aanwezig is;
b. indien het een arbeidsplaats betreft waarvan de beschikbaarheid niet ten minste vijf weken voor het indienen van de aanvraag aan het Uitvoeringsinstituut werknemersverzekeringen is gemeld;
c. indien de werkgever niet kan aantonen voldoende inspanningen te hebben gepleegd de arbeidsplaats door prioriteitgenietend aanbod op de arbeidsmarkt te vervullen:

18 Wet arbeid vreemdelingen, available at http://wetten.overheid.nl/BWBR0007149 [last accessed on 24 January 2014].

d. indien van de te vervullen arbeidsplaats de arbeidsvoorwaarden, arbeidsverhoudingen of arbeidsomstandigheden beneden het niveau liggen dat wettelijk is vereist of in de desbetreffende bedrijfstak gebruikelijk is;
e. indien het een vreemdeling betreft:
1°. die niet beschikt over een voor het verrichten van arbeid geldige verblijfsvergunning, noch een zodanige vergunning heeft aangevraagd, noch, voor zover ter verkrijging van een dergelijke vergunning vereist, een machtiging tot voorlopig verblijf heeft aangevraagd, dan wel
2°. aan wie een verblijfsvergunning is geweigerd of wiens verblijfsvergunning is ingetrokken;
f. indien het een vreemdeling betreft, die met de desbetreffende arbeid over een periode van een maand niet ten minste een bedrag verdient gelijk aan het minimumloon, bedoeld in artikel 8, eerste lid, onderdeel a, van de Wet minimumloon en minimumvakantiebijslag;
g. indien het een arbeidsplaats betreft die behoort tot een bij algemene maatregel van bestuur aangewezen categorie van werkzaamheden, waarvan het niet in het Nederlands belang is deze door vreemdelingen te laten verrichten; of
h. indien het een categorie van werkzaamheden of van vreemdelingen betreft waarvoor overeenkomstig artikel 5a een limiet aan het aantal te verlenen tewerkstellingsvergunningen is gesteld, welke limiet is bereikt.
[...]

3. In door Onze Minister te bepalen gevallen kan:
a. in buitengewone omstandigheden worden afgeweken van het eerste lid, onder b;
b. ten behoeve van de bevordering van internationale handelscontacten of in het kader van de uitoefening van een geestelijke, godsdienstige of levensbeschouwelijke functie worden afgeweken van het eerste lid, onder a, b, c en f;

Wet op de collectieve arbeidsovereenkomst of 24 December 1927[19]

Artikel 1
[...]
3. Nietig is het beding, waarbij een werkgever verplicht wordt arbeiders van een bepaald ras of met een bepaalde godsdienst, levensbeschouwelijke of

19 Wet op de collectieve arbeidsovereenkomst, available at http://wetten.overheid.nl/BWBR0001937 [last accessed on 2 January 2014].

politieke overtuiging of leden van een bepaalde vereniging in dienst te nemen of waarbij hij zich verplicht, te weigeren hen in dienst te nemen.

Arbeidsomstandighedenwet[20]

Artikel 3

[...]

2. De werkgever voert, binnen het algemeen arbeidsomstandighedenbeleid, een beleid gericht op voorkoming en indien dat niet mogelijk is beperking van psychosociale arbeidsbelasting.

Jurisprudence

Case 1

The Court adjudicated on the character of labour relations between an imam (who was dismissed) and his employer, an Islamic foundation. Despite the fact that the imam was not subject to any instructions regarding the conduct of his religious duties as religious minister, other requirements and conditions were applied by the employer, e.g. with regard to working hours and vacation regulations. In the Court's opinion, the relationship between the two parties was therefore based on a power relation, which involved the legal protection of the imam in the light of labour law. (Hoge Raad, 17 June 1994, JAR 1994, 152)

Case 2

Behaviour which does not conform to the commonly acknowledged patterns of social co-existence in the Netherlands, such as the refusal to shake hands with people of the opposite sex, may form the basis for an employee's dismissal or the rejection of a candidate for a job in a public office. Despite the fact that a refusal to shake hands can be recognised as a direct expression of one's religious beliefs and convictions (in this case it was argued by the orthodox interpretation of Islamic norms), the custom of shaking hands is treated in the Netherlands as a traditional form of greeting. This also forms the commonly acknowledged pattern of behaviour in the public arena, primarily with regard to public offices whose representatives are expected to respect both the state's neutrality and the principle of equality between men and women. (Gerechtshof 's-

20 Arbeidsomstandighedenwet, available at http://wetten.overheid.nl/BWBR0010346 [last accessed on 2 January 2014].

Gravenhage, 10 April 2012, ECLI:NL:GHSGR:2012:BW1270[21] which confirmed the adjudication of the Rechtbank Rotterdam, 6 August 2008, ECLI:NL:RBROT:2008: BD9643[22])

10.2 Religious Holidays and Trade Regulations

One of the issues relevant to the present context concerns the regulation of holidays in the Netherlands, which may occasionally lead to certain perplexities in the case of non-Christian denominations. The first legislative regulations in this regard appeared in 1907, when the Act on Labour Agreements (Wet op de Arbeidsovereenkomst) was introduced, followed in 1919 by the Working Hours Act (Arbeidstijdenwet, hereafter ATW) concerning employees' right to (religious) holidays. Art. 5:1 of the ATW defines the right to such holidays on days other than Sundays (e.g. Art. 5:1). A ban on Sunday work (with the exception of legally listed cases) was laid down in the ATW of 1995, which protects the right to free Sundays and other rest days. In 2001 the law was amended on the basis of the Bussemaker/ Van Dijke Act, which added article 5.4 (current Art. 5:6) to the ATW.[23] As set out in Art. 5:6 of the ATW, each employee is guaranteed at least thirteen Sundays free from work, unless other agreements between an employee and an employer have been signed. Work on Sunday is permitted if it is justified by the character of the work (such as production lines, public transport, medical care, police forces) or a company's specific situation (e.g. an extensive project that requires additional effort). Moreover, often the agreement of bodies representing employees' rights is also required.[24] The ATW does not envisage the same guarantees for other days of the week, which would meet the needs of non-Christian denominations. In this regard, it appears that the Dutch system of law is based on traditional rather than religious grounds.[25]

21 Available at http://uitspraken.rechtspraak.nl/inziendocument?id=ECLI:NL:GHSGR:2012: BW1270 [last accessed on 9 February 2014].

22 Available at http://uitspraken.rechtspraak.nl/inziendocument?id=ECLI:NL:RBROT:2008: BD9643 [last accessed on 9 February 2014].

23 See more in Fluiten, Zondag, 'Godsdienst in arbeidsverhoudingen', pp. 431–432; Wet van 14 maart 2003 tot wijziging van de Arbeidstijdenwet en het Burgerlijk Wetboek ter verruiming van zeggenschap van werknemers over arbeidstijden, available at http://www .eerstekamer.nl/behandeling/20030410/publicatie_wet/document3/f=/w27224st.pdf [last accessed on 25 January 2014].

24 Fluiten, Zondag, 'Godsdienst in arbeidsverhoudingen', p. 432.

25 See also Sunday Law (Zondagswet), Art. 2, Art. 3 and Art. 5, available at http://wetten .overheid.nl/BWBR0002120 [last accessed on 24 January 2014].

Among religious traditions, only Christian holidays have been incorporated in the Dutch calendar of officially recognised rest days, i.e.: Good Friday, Easter, Ascension Day, Whitsun and Christmas.[26] The legislator envisages however that an employer may give permission for a free day during other religious holidays or ceremonies. This legal opportunity is not binding, and an employer has the right to refuse. Nevertheless, an employer is obliged to set the same criteria regarding the representatives of diverse denominations and to provide sufficient argument in cases of refusal.[27]

It should be noted that the regulations regarding rest days and religious holidays also refer to the conditions of trade. As set out in Art. 2a and Art. 2b of the Act on Shop Trading Hours (*Winkeltijdenwet*, hereafter Wtw) of 1996, as amended,[28] trading on Sundays and official rest days is forbidden unless permission is given by the Municipal Council (Art. 3). However, Art. 6 of the Wtw provides the possibility to adjust this principle to the followers of other denominations through the replacement of the rest days listed in Art. 2 by other holidays in accordance with a shop owner's religious beliefs.

Arbeidstijdenwet, 23 November 1995[29]

Hoofdstuk 5. Arbeids- en rusttijden

§ 5.1. Algemene bepalingen
Gelijkstelling met de zondag

Artikel 5:1
1. Dit hoofdstuk en de daarop berustende bepalingen vinden ten aanzien van de zondag voor werknemers, die in verband met hun godsdienstige of levensbeschouwelijke opvattingen, de wekelijkse rustdag op een andere dag dan de zondag vieren, overeenkomstige toepassing voor die dag in plaats van ten aanzien van de zondag, indien die werknemers een daartoe strekkend schriftelijk verzoek tot de werkgever hebben gericht.
2. Elk beding waarbij wordt afgeweken van het eerste lid, is nietig
[...]

26 Loenen, *Geloof in het geding ...*, p. 66.

27 Fluiten, Zondag, 'Godsdienst in arbeidsverhoudingen', p. 433. See also HR 30 maart 1984, NJ 1984, 350.

28 The amendment of the Wtw of 11 June 2013 (in force since 1 July 2013) extended the scope of municipal authorities' competences.

29 Arbeidstijdenwet, available at http://wetten.overheid.nl/BWBR0007671 [last accessed on 24 January 2014].

Artikel 5:3
1. De werkgever organiseert de arbeid zodanig, dat de jeugdige werknemer een onafgebroken rusttijd heeft van ten minste 12 uren in elke aaneengesloten periode van 24 uren, waarin zijn begrepen de uren tussen 23.00 uur en 06.00 uur.
2. De werkgever organiseert de arbeid zodanig, dat de werknemer van 18 jaar of ouder een onafgebroken rusttijd heeft van ten minste 11 uren in elke aaneengesloten periode van 24 uren, welke rusttijd eenmaal in elke aaneengesloten periode van 7 maal 24 uren mag worden ingekort tot ten minste 8 uren, indien de aard van de arbeid of de bedrijfsomstandigheden dit met zich brengen.
3. De in het eerste of tweede lid bedoelde periode vangt aan op het eerste tijdstip van de dag, waarop de werknemer arbeid verricht.
[...]

Artikel 5:6
1. De werkgever organiseert de arbeid zodanig, dat de werknemer op zondag geen arbeid verricht, behalve voor zover dat uit de aard van de arbeid voortvloeit en het tegendeel is bedongen.
2. Indien de bedrijfsomstandigheden dit noodzakelijk maken, kan van het eerste lid worden afgeweken, indien de werkgever daartoe overeenstemming heeft bereikt met het medezeggenschapsorgaan of, bij het ontbreken daarvan, met de belanghebbende werknemers. De werknemer verricht in de omstandigheden, bedoeld in de vorige zin, uitsluitend arbeid op zondag, indien hij daarmee voor dat geval instemt.
3. De werkgever organiseert de arbeid zodanig, dat de werknemer op ten minste 13 zondagen in elke periode van 52 aaneengesloten weken geen arbeid verricht.
4. Bij collectieve regeling kan van het derde lid worden afgeweken, met inachtneming van:
a. het eerste lid, of
b. het tweede lid.
Bij toepassing van de aanhef en onderdeel a van de vorige zin, verricht de werknemer uitsluitend op 40 of meer zondagen in elke periode van 52 aaneengesloten weken arbeid, indien hij daarmee voor dat geval instemt. Elk beding, waarbij op een andere wijze dan in dit lid is bepaald, wordt afgeweken van het derde lid, is nietig.

Arbeidstijdenbesluit, 4 December 1995[30]

Artikel 4.2:1
1. In afwijking van de artikelen 5:7, tweede lid, onder a, en 5:8, eerste lid, van de wet kan dit artikel worden toegepast.
2. De werkgever organiseert de arbeid voorafgaand aan Nieuwjaarsdag, de Christelijke Eerste of Tweede Paasdag, de dag waarop de verjaardag van de Koning wordt gevierd, Hemelvaartsdag, de Christelijke Eerste of Tweede Pinksterdag, 5 december en de Eerste of Tweede Kerstdag zodanig dat de werknemer van 18 jaar of ouder in de aaneengesloten periode van 7 dagen voorafgaand aan die dag ten hoogste 2 maal 14 uren per dienst onderscheidenlijk per nachtdienst arbeid verricht, indien de aard van de arbeid of de bedrijfsomstandigheden dit in verband met die feestdag met zich brengen.
3. Indien een door godsdienstige of levensbeschouwelijke opvattingen ingegeven andere dag dan een dag als bedoeld in het tweede lid de aard van de arbeid of de bedrijfsomstandigheden beïnvloedt op een wijze die gelijkenis vertoont met de beïnvloeding van een in dat lid bedoelde dag, is dat lid van overeenkomstige toepassing.

Winkeltijdenwet of 21 March 1996[31]

Artikel 2
1. Het is verboden een winkel voor het publiek geopend te hebben:
a. op zondag;
b. op Nieuwjaarsdag, op Goede Vrijdag na 19 uur, op tweede Paasdag, op Hemelvaartsdag, op tweede Pinksterdag, op 24 december na 19 uur, op eerste en tweede Kerstdag en op 4 mei na 19 uur;
c. op werkdagen voor 6 uur en na 22 uur.
2. Het is voorts verboden op de in het eerste lid bedoelde dagen en tijden in de uitoefening van een bedrijf, anders dan in een winkel, goederen te koop aan te bieden of te verkopen aan en in rechtstreekse aanraking met particulieren.

Artikel 3
1. De gemeenteraad kan bij verordening vrijstelling verlenen van de in artikel 2 vervatte verboden.

30 Arbeidstijdenbesluit, available at http://wetten.overheid.nl/BWBR0007687 [last accessed on 24 January 2014].
31 Winkeltijdenwet, available at http://wetten.overheid.nl/BWBR0007952 [last accessed on 25 January 2014].

2. De gemeenteraad kan bij verordening aan burgemeester en wethouders de bevoegdheid verlenen om in de gevallen, in de verordening aan te wijzen, en met inachtneming van de daarin gestelde regels op daartoe strekkend verzoek ontheffing van de in het eerste lid bedoelde verboden te verlenen.
3. De vrijstellingen en ontheffingen kunnen onder beperkingen worden verleend. Aan de vrijstellingen en ontheffingen kunnen voorschriften worden verbonden.
[...]

Artikel 6
1. Indien de eigenaar of beheerder van een winkel tot een kerkgenootschap behoort, dat de wekelijkse rustdag op een andere dag dan de zondag houdt, of te goeder trouw verklaart een godsdienst of levensovertuiging te belijden welke vordert, dat de wekelijkse rustdag op een andere dag dan de zondag wordt gehouden, verlenen burgemeester en wethouders op zijn verzoek ontheffing van het verbod van artikel 2, eerste lid, onder a.
2. Aan de ontheffing wordt het voorschrift verbonden dat de winkel op die andere dag gesloten dient te zijn.
[...]

Artikel 8
1. Bij algemene maatregel van bestuur kan vrijstelling worden verleend van de in artikel 2 vervatte verboden ten behoeve van:
a. instellingen voor de volksgezondheid,
b. het verkeer en het vervoer en
c. de verkoop van nieuwsbladen en tijdschriften.
2. De vrijstellingen kunnen onder beperkingen worden verleend. Aan de vrijstellingen kunnen voorschriften worden verbonden.

Jurisprudence

Case 1

The Dutch catalogue of official bank holidays cannot be extended by the inclusion of other, e.g. non-Christian religious holidays. Such holidays do not have an equal position with the rest days which have been traditionally encompassed and acknowledged in the Dutch system of law. (HR 30 maart 1984, NJ 1984, 350)

CHAPTER 11

Islamic Slaughter

Issues regarding ritual slaughter have been widely discussed in Dutch public debate, leading to legislative developments which explicitly refer to Islamic communities. Legal regulations and issues under discussion at a parliamentary level have pertained to religious freedom and animal rights, as well as the mutual relations between these two tenets. The delicacy and somewhat controversial nature of the issue have contributed to the broad and detailed legislation in this regard.

Both Islamic and Jewish traditions exclude the use of stunning prior to the (ritual) cutting of the throat. Until 1982 Dutch Muslims had not been allowed to slaughter animals in accordance with their religious prescriptions, while this right had been given to Jews.[1] It appears that in the 1980s the political climate (the activity of radical right-wing, Islam-sceptical parties in particular) influenced the shape of the debate.[2] On the other hand, one should consider the role of the European Convention for the Protection of Animals for Slaughter of 1979, which envisages certain (religiously justified) exceptions to the principle of the compulsory stunning of animals.[3]

One of the controversies in the Dutch debate pertained to the export of meat from ritual slaughter, which could not be justified by religious arguments. Nevertheless, the right to export was retained due to strong protest among Jewish and Islamic circles.[4] The issue reappeared in further parliamentary discussions.

Considering the Dutch system of law, one should refer to the constitutional principle of religious freedom (Art. 6 of the Dutch Constitution), which forms the general foundation of further regulations. However, the Constitution in no part directly refers to the issue of ritual slaughter nor to any other food regulations. The general frameworks concerning the humane treatment of animals for slaughter are included in the Act on Animals (Wet dieren, hereafter

1 Nhass, Hanan, 'Mogen moslims in Nederland ritueel slachten?' in *Multicultureel Nederland in 70 vragen*, Tazelaar, C.A. (Houten: Bohn Staffen Van Loghum, 2002), pp. 94–95.

2 See Shadid, Wasif A.R., Koningsveld, Peter S. van (eds.), *Islam in Dutch Society: Current Developments and Future Prospects* (Kampen: Kok, 1992), p. 20.

3 Rath, Jan, Penninx, Rinus, Groenendijk, Kees, Meyer, Astrid, *Western Europe and its Islam* (Leiden: Koninklijke Brill NV, 2001), pp. 58–59.

4 Rath, Penninx, Groenendijk, Meyer, *Western Europe and its Islam*, p. 60.

Wd) of 2011. The Wd, which in Art. 2.10 precisely defines the conditions of slaughtering, has exempted Islamic and Jewish practices from the scope of its legal relevance (Art. 2.10 §4 and Art. 2.10 §5). According to the Wd, the conditions of ritual slaughter can be further defined in other implementing regulations.

The Regulation on Ritual Slughter (Besluit ritueel slachten, hereafter Brs) of 1996, as amended, directly and exclusively refers to Jewish and Islamic religious traditions (Art. 2) regarding the conditions of slaughtering animals with no prior stunning. According to Art. 4.1 and Art. 5 of the Brs, it aims to implement fully Regulation (EC) No. 1099/2009 of 24 September 2009 (in force since 1 January 2013). Art. 8 of the Brs specifies the time frame during which an animal should be restrained during the process of slaughtering, i.e. 45 seconds with regard to cattle, and 30 seconds in the case of sheep and goats.[5]

Regarding ritual slaughter issues one should also refer to the the Covenant of Ritual Slaughter with no Prior Stunning (Convenant onbedwelmd slachten volgens religieuze riten, hereafter Covenant). The Covenant has been defined as an agreement requiring further legislative regulations, as set out in Art. 2.2. The same legislative path is expected for the required formal registration (which is to replace the former requirement of reporting) of slaughterhouses (Art. 2.3 and Art. 2.4). With regard to both Jewish and Islamic communities, the selection of slaughterhouses which would be permitted to slaughter animals with no prior stunning is to be performed at the request of the respective representatives (in the case of Islamic communities this is the Commission of Islamic Slaughter of the CMO, i.e. the Commissie Islamitisch Slachten van het Contactorgaan Moslims en Overheid). Further regulations have also been envisaged with regard to the education required in order to carry out ritual slaughter (Art. 3).

The Covenant does not have the legal rank of e.g. a ministerial regulation. The document was signed by the State Secretary in the Ministry of Economic Affairs (Henk Bleker), the representative of the Association of Abattoirs and Meat-Packing Companies (de Vereniging van Slachterijen en Vleesverwerkende bedrijven), the CMO, and the General Permanent Commission of the Dutch-Israelite Community (de Permanente Commissie tot de Algemene Zaken van het Nederlands-Israëlitisch Kerkgenootschap), and came into force on 6 June 2012.[6] The Covenant was aimed at meeting the requirements of Reg-

5 Art. 9 includes sheep, goats and poultry.

6 http://www.rijksoverheid.nl/nieuws/2012/11/01/regels-ritueel-slachten-naar-tweede-kamer.html [last accessed on 2 June 2014]. The text of the Covenant is available at https://www

ulation (EC) No. 1099/2009 on the protection of animals at the time of killing (in force since 1 January 2013).[7]

The significant provision has been placed in Art. 2 of the Covenant with regard to the loss of an animal's consciousness. Here, the main stipulation concerns a time period of 40 seconds from the moment of the cut, which may partly correspond to Art. 8 of the Brs. However, the Brs refers only to the restraining of an animal, which should last 30 or 45 seconds, depending on the species, and it does not define the time frame within which an animal should lose its consciousness. Art. 2 § 1a of the Covenant lists the physiological indicators which confirm the loss of an animal's consciousness. When at least three indicators cannot be observed, intervention is required in order to stun the animal. Art. 2 also defines the throat cut (Art. 2 § 1b), the knife (Art. 2 § 1c) and the process of slaughtering (Art. 2 § 1d) including the restraining (Art. 2 § 1e). Relative autonomy has been given to the performers of slaughter regarding the use of specified methods and the decision to slaughter with no prior stunning (Art. 2.1d). In the Covenant, the conditions of the proper restraining of animals have also been laid down in a detailed manner (Art. 2.1e). Contrary to Art. 8 of the Brs, the Covenant does not provide any time frame regarding the restraining, but it stipulates that the animal should be restrained until it has completely lost consciousness.

.eerstekamer.nl/overig/20120607/convenant_onbedwelmd_slachten/document [last accessed on 6 August 2013]. Although the Covenant does not have binding force in a legislative sense, it is an official agreement in force, and it is therefore included in this chapter.

7 On 1 November 2012, the draft of the new law was forwarded to the Tweede Kamer, i.e. Besluit van 12 november 2012, nr. 12.002291, tot wijziging van het Besluit doden van dieren en het Besluit ritueel slachten in verband met de uitvoering van Verordening (EG) nr. 1099/2009 inzake de bescherming van dieren bij het doden (Pb EU 2009, L 303), available at http://www.rijksoverheid.nl/bestanden/documenten-en-publicaties/besluiten/2012/11/19/besluit-over-bescherming-van-dieren-bij-het-doden/besluit-over-bescherming-van-dieren-bij-het-doden.pdf [last accessed on 2 June 2014]. The draft is based on the provisions of the Covenant and Regulation (EC) no, 1099/2009. The draft includes the requirement of the registration of slaughterhouses (Art. 6.5 and 6.5 a–e) and their monitoring and control (Art. 6.5 f), defines the conditions of restraint (Art. 6.7 a–b), the cut (6.8) and the period an animal may remain conscious for (Art. 6.8 a). The draft is aimed at the fulfilment of the principle of religious freedom, as noted in the included elucidation—Nota van Toelichting, available at http://www.rijksoverheid.nl/documenten-en-publicaties/kamerstukken/2012/11/01/aanbiedingsbrief-bij-ontwerpbesluit-rond-het-doden-van-dieren-zonder-voorafgaande-bedwelming.html [last accessed on 2 June 2014].

Wet dieren, 19 May 2011[8]

Artikel 2.10. Doden van dieren

1. Het is verboden om dieren behorend tot bij algemene maatregel van bestuur aangewezen diersoorten of diercategorieën te doden, behoudens in gevallen waarin een dier wordt gedood voor de bedrijfsmatige productie van dierlijke producten of in andere dan bij of krachtens algemene maatregel van bestuur aangewezen gevallen.

2. Bij of krachtens algemene maatregel van bestuur worden regels gesteld voor de uitvoering van bindende onderdelen van EG-maatregelen over het doden, het bedwelmen, het fixeren, het onderbrengen en het verplaatsen van dieren.

3. Bij of krachtens algemene maatregel van bestuur kunnen voor het onderwerp, bedoeld in het tweede lid, regels worden gesteld voor bij deze maatregel aan te wijzen diersoorten of diercategorieën die betrekking hebben op onder meer:

a. een verbod op het doden van bepaalde dieren;
b. de wijze waarop dieren worden gedood;
c. situaties waarin het is toegestaan dieren te doden;
d. voorwaarden waaronder het is toegestaan dieren te doden;
e. de personen die dieren doden, of die daarbij betrokken zijn;
f. de plaats waar dieren worden gedood;
g. het vervoeren, het aanvoeren en het afvoeren van dieren naar de plaats waar wordt gedood;
h. het verplaatsen van dieren in de ruimten waar dieren worden gedood;
i. het onderbrengen van dieren in de ruimten waar dieren worden gedood;
j. het fixeren van dieren;
k. het bedwelmen van dieren;
l. de inrichting, uitvoering en vormgeving van ruimten waar dieren worden gedood, waaronder de aanwezige voorzieningen;
m. de gegevens over de te doden dieren die voorafgaand aan het doden worden overgelegd;
n. de gezondheidsstatus van de te doden dieren;
o. de onderzoeken aan en met betrekking tot de dieren;
p. de keuring van dieren;
q. de personen die dieren keuren, of die daarbij betrokken zijn;
r. hygiëne, het voorkomen van de verspreiding van dierziekten, zoönosen en ziekteverschijnselen, en het weren van ziekteverwekkers, en

8 Wet dieren, available at http://wetten.overheid.nl/BWBR0030250 [last accessed on 2 June 2014].

s. de instrumenten, installaties en verdere voorzieningen voor het fixeren, bedwelmen of doden van dieren.
4. Het is toegestaan om dieren zonder voorafgaande bedwelming te doden volgens de israëlitische of de islamitische ritus. Bij algemene maatregel van bestuur worden in het belang van de bescherming van de dieren nadere regels gesteld over het doden volgens de israëlitische of de islamitische ritus.
5. De regels, bedoeld in het vierde lid, kunnen betrekking hebben op onder meer:
a. de wijze waarop dieren worden gedood;
b. de personen die het doden van dieren uitvoeren;
c. de inrichting, uitvoering en vormgeving van ruimten waar dieren worden gedood, waaronder de aanwezige voorzieningen, en
d. de aanwezigheid van een op grond van artikel 8.1 aangewezen ambtenaar, tevens zijnde een dierenarts, en de door die ambtenaar te geven aanwijzingen.

Gezondheids- en welzijnswet voor dieren, 24 September 1992[9]

Artikel 44
1. Bij of krachtens algemene maatregel van bestuur worden regelen gesteld omtrent het doden van dieren van bij die maatregel aangewezen soorten of categorieën van dieren.
2. De krachtens het eerste lid gestelde regelen hebben in ieder geval betrekking op:
– de wijze waarop, de situaties waarin en de personen door wie dieren mogen worden gedood;
– de bedwelming van slachtdieren;
– de bedrijfsuitrusting en installatie in slachterijen.
3. Het slachten van dieren zonder voorafgaande bedwelming volgens de israëlitische of de islamitische ritus is toegestaan.
4. Het slachten, bedoeld in het derde lid, mag slechts geschieden in door Onze Minister, in overeenstemming met Onze Minister van Volksgezondheid, Welzijn en Sport aan te wijzen inrichtingen.
5. Een aanwijzing als bedoeld in het vierde lid vindt plaats:
a. indien het betreft het slachten volgens de israëlitische ritus: op verzoek van de Permanente Commissie tot de Algemene Zaken van het Nederlands-Israëlitisch Kerkgenootschap;

9 Gezondheids- en welzijnswet voor dieren, available at http://wetten.overheid.nl/BWBR0005662 [last accessed on 2 June 2014].

b. indien het betreft het slachten volgens de islamitische ritus: op verzoek van één of meer organisaties die geacht kunnen worden alle of een bepaalde groep islamieten in Nederland te vertegenwoordigen; een en ander voor zover uit het desbetreffende verzoek blijkt dat in het deel van het land dat vanuit de aan te wijzen inrichtingen pleegt te worden bediend behoefte bestaat aan vlees, afkomstig van volgens de desbetreffende ritus geslachte dieren.
6. Een aanwijzing als bedoeld in het vierde lid vindt voorts plaats op verzoek van een israëlitische of islamitische groepering in een ander land, waarmee wordt ingestemd door de in het vijfde lid, onderdeel a, genoemde commissie, onderscheidenlijk de in onderdeel b bedoelde organisaties indien in het verzoek wordt aangetoond dat bij die israëlitische of islamitische groepering behoefte bestaat aan de import van vlees afkomstig van volgens de desbetreffende ritus geslachte dieren.
7. Onze Minister stelt, in overeenstemming met Onze Minister van Volksgezondheid, Welzijn en Sport en in overleg met de aangewezen inrichting en
a. voor zover het betreft de behoefte aan vlees, afkomstig van volgens de israëlitische ritus geslachte dieren: in overleg met de Permanente Commissie tot de Algemene Zaken van het Nederlands-Israëlitisch Kerkgenootschap, of
b. voor zover het betreft de behoefte aan vlees, afkomstig van volgens de islamitische ritus geslachte dieren: in overleg met de in het vijfde lid, onderdeel b, bedoelde organisaties, het aantal in een bepaald tijdvak per inrichting ritueel te slachten dieren vast, waarmede in de bedoelde behoefte aan vlees kan worden voorzien.
8. Het slachten zonder voorafgaande bedwelming mag slechts geschieden:
a. voor zover het betreft het slachten volgens de israëlitische ritus: door personen die daartoe door het Opperrabbinaat voor Nederland zijn gemachtigd, en
b. voor zover het betreft het slachten volgens de islamitische ritus: door personen die daartoe door de in het vijfde lid, onderdeel b, bedoelde organisaties zijn aangewezen, mits die personen daarvan door een schriftelijk bewijs aan de keuringsdierenarts hebben doen blijken.
Deze personen voegen zich ten aanzien van het aantal door hen ritueel te slachten dieren naar de voor elke inrichting aangewezen hoeveelheid; zij volgen ter zake de aanwijzingen van de keuringsdierenarts op, die toeziet, dat het vastgestelde aantal niet wordt overschreden.
9. Bij algemene maatregel van bestuur worden in het belang van de bescherming van het slachtdier regelen gesteld omtrent het slachten volgens de israëlitische of de islamitische ritus.
10. Een voordracht voor een algemene maatregel van bestuur als bedoeld in het negende lid wordt Ons gedaan door Onze Minister en Onze Minister van Volksgezondheid, Welzijn en Sport.

Besluit ritueel slachten, 6 November 1996[10]

Artikel 1
In dit besluit wordt verstaan onder:
– *Verordening* (EG) *nr. 1099/2009*: Verordening (EG) nr. 1099/2009 van de Raad van 24 september 2009 inzake de bescherming van dieren bij het doden (PbEU 2009, L 303);
– *wet*: Gezondheids- en welzijnswet voor dieren.
Artikel 1a
Dit besluit berust mede op de artikelen 44, eerste en tweede lid, van de Gezondheids-en welzijnswet voor dieren.

Artikel 2
Dit besluit is van toepassing op dieren die zonder voorafgaande bedwelming worden geslacht volgens de israëlitische of de islamitische ritus.

Artikel 3
Het is verboden te handelen in strijd met bij ministeriële regeling aan te wijzen artikelen van Verordening (EG) nr. 1099/2009.

Artikel 4
1. Bij ministeriële regeling worden regels gesteld voor een goede uitvoering van Verordening (EG) nr. 1099/2009.
2. De regels, bedoeld in het eerste lid, kunnen betrekking hebben op:
a. het aanwijzen van een bevoegde autoriteit;
b. het verstrekken, schorsen en intrekken van getuigschriften van vakbekwaamheid;

10 Besluit ritueel slachten, available at http://wetten.overheid.nl/BWBR0008316 [last accessed on 2 June 2014]. The order refers merely to Islamic and Jewish traditions. General rules and conditions for the slaughter of animals are defined in Besluit doden van dieren of 16 May 1997, which does not however refer to animals slaughtered in accordance with Islamic and Jewish practices, available at http://wetten.overheid.nl/BWBR0008686 [last accessed on 2 June 2014]. Other rules have also been included in the Besluit houders van dieren, available at http://www.rijksoverheid.nl/documenten-en-publicaties/besluiten/2012/06/14/besluit-houdende-regels-met-betrekking-tot-houders-van-dieren.html [last accessed on 26 December 2013]. See also the amendment of 1 November 2012, available at http://www.rijksoverheid.nl/documenten-en-publicaties/besluiten/2012/11/01/voorhang-ontwerpbesluit-wijziging-besluit-houders-van-dieren-inzake-wijzigingen-rond-het-doden-van-dieren-zonder-voorafgaande-bedwelming.html [last accessed on 2 June 2014].

c. het goedkeuren van opleidingsprogramma's en de inhoud en uitvoeringsbepalingen van examens;
d. het uitvoeren van controles en inspectie die relevant zijn voor de bescherming van dieren bij het doden en met het doden verband houdende activiteiten;
e. gidsen voor goede praktijken.

Artikel 5
1. Het onbedwelmd slachten van dieren geschiedt overeenkomstig de door de op grond van artikel 114, eerste lid, van de wet[11] aangewezen toezichthouders in het belang van de bescherming van het dier gegeven aanwijzingen.
2. De in het eerste lid bedoelde aanwijzingen kunnen betrekking hebben op:
– de gang van zaken rond het slachtproces, daaronder mede verstaan de wijze waarop en de volgorde waarin dieren worden aangeboden voor de slacht;
– het aantal personen dat betrokken dient te zijn bij het fixeren, slachten en verbloeden van het dier;
– het staken van het slachtproces indien onvoldoende is gegarandeerd dat daarbij wordt voldaan aan de eisen van Verordening (EG) nr. 1099/2009 en van dit besluit.
3. Onverminderd het tweede lid mag, naast de bij de slachthandelingen betrokken personen en de personen die tijdens de slachthandelingen de israëlitische of islamitische ritus verrichten, ten hoogste één persoon bij het slachten aanwezig zijn.
[...]

Artikel 8
1. Runderen worden gefixeerd door middel van een toestel dat is voorzien van een tijd-mechanisme dat gedurende 45 seconden na het bedienen daarvan, de opheffing van de fixatie onmogelijk maakt; dit mechanisme wordt onmiddellijk na het toebrengen van de halssnede in werking gesteld.
2. Na het toebrengen van de halssnede blijven schapen en geiten gedurende tenminste dertig seconden gefixeerd in de positie die de dieren innamen op het moment van het toebrengen van de halssnede.

Artikel 9
1. Het toebrengen van de halssnede gebeurt met een vlijmscherp mes door een persoon die niet tevens belast is met het fixeren van de dieren.

11 I.e. Gezondheids- en welzijnswet voor dieren.

2. Bij schapen, geiten en pluimvee worden ten minste gedurende 30 seconden en bij runderen ten minste gedurende 45 seconden na het aanbrengen van de halssnede geen verdere slachthandelingen verricht.

Convenant onbedwelmd slachten volgens religieuze riten, 5 June 2012[12]

Artikel 2 (afspraken over normen ter verbetering van het dierenwelzijn)
1. Convenantspartijen onderschrijven de volgende normen:
a. bewusteloosheid:
1°. Binnen een periode van 40 seconden vanaf het moment van het aanbrengen van de halssnede wordt door de slachter getest of het dier het bewustzijn heeft verloren aan de hand van de hierna genoemde indicatoren. Voor de vaststelling van de bewusteloosheid kunnen de volgende indicatoren worden gebruikt, waarbij ten minste drie van de genoemde indicatoren als negatief worden beoordeeld:
– spontane ooglidreflex;
– pijnprikkel neustussenschot;
– spontane ritmische ademhalingen;
– oprichtreflex
– dreigreflex.
2°. Ingeval een dier nog bij bewustzijn is na verloop van het verstrijken van de periode van 40 seconden, genoemd in onder 1°, na het moment van het aanbrengen van de halssnede, wordt het dier onverwijld bedwelmd door middel van een extra ingreep.
b. halssnede: de halssnede wordt met een ononderbroken, vloeiende beweging uitgevoerd, met als doel het dier zo snel mogelijk te verbloeden.
c. mes:
1°. het te gebruiken mes is te allen tijde zeer scherp en gaaf en wordt na iedere snede gereinigd;
2°. de lengte van het mes is minimaal anderhalf tot twee keer de breedte van de snijoppervlakte.
d. Tot aan het moment waarop convenantspartijen nadere afspraken hebben gemaakt, op basis van het advies van de wetenschappelijke adviescommissie, over de geschiktheid van het dier qua type, omvang gewicht en mentale

12 Convenant onbedwelmd slachten volgens religieuze riten, available at https://www.eerstekamer.nl/overig/20120607/convenant_onbedwelmd_slachten/document [last accessed on 2 June 2014].

toestand om onbedwelmd te worden geslacht volgens religieuze riten, is het aan de slachter om te bepalen of het dier qua type, omvang, gewicht en mentale toestand geschikt is om onbedwelmd te worden geslacht volgens religieuze riten.
e. de duur en de methode van fixatie van een dier:
1°. de fixatie van het te doden dier wordt niet eerder opgeheven dan nadat bij de bewusteloosheidstest vast is komen te staan dat het dier definitief buiten bewustzijn is;
2°. het hoofd en lichaam van dieren die onbedwelmd worden geslacht worden mechanisch gefixeerd, waarbij voor het hoofd van schapen en geiten ook handmatige fixatie is toegestaan;
3°. het fixatieapparaat:
– verkeert in een goede staat;
– bevat geen scherpe uitsteeksels;
– bestaat uit soepel bewegende delen, zonder dat schokkende bewegingen agitatie bij het dier kunnen veroorzaken;
– veroorzaakt geen geluiden die stress veroorzaken bij het dier;
– is geschikt voor het te doden dier;
– houdt het dier voor en tijdens de fixatie in een comfortabele positie, waarbij het apparaat voldoende druk kan uitoefenen om het dier gefixeerd te houden, zonder daarbij onnodige stress te veroorzaken;
– beschikt over een vloer die antislip is en dieren mogen net voor en tijdens de fixatie op geen enkele wijze kunnen uitglijden.
4°. het dier gaat de fixatiebox niet eerder binnen dan nadat de slachter gereed staat met het mes om het dier te doden;
5°. Wanneer dieren een te dikke vacht hebben waardoor de halssnede minder makkelijk kan worden uitgevoerd dan normaal, wordt de hals van het dier eerst geschoren of de wol gescheiden ter plaatse van de snede.
2. De Staatssecretaris zal zich inspannen om te komen tot regelgeving waarin de normen, bedoeld in het eerste lid, zijn vastgelegd.
3. In aanvulling op het tweede lid, zal de Staatssecretaris zich inspannen om te komen tot regelgeving met betrekking tot een verplichte registratie van slachthuizen alvorens zij onbedwelmd mogen slachten volgens religieuze riten, welke kan worden geschorst dan wel ingetrokken als niet wordt voldaan aan voorbedoelde regelgeving of andere voorschriften die aan de slachthuizen worden gesteld, in plaats van de huidige meldingsplicht.
4. In aanvulling op het tweede en derde lid, zal de Staatssecretaris zich inspannen om te komen tot regelgeving met betrekking tot de onderwerpen, bedoeld in artikel 4, negende lid, na overleg met en na instemming van convenantspartijen, genoemd in de aanhef, onder 2 tot en met 4.

5. In aanvulling op het tweede, derde en vierde lid, zal de Staatssecretaris zich inspannen om in de uitvoeringsregelgeving op grond van de Wet dieren vast te leggen dat de aanwijzing van slachthuizen en slachters die onbedwelmd mogen slachten volgens de israëlitische of de islamitische ritus plaatsvindt:
a. indien het betreft aanwijzen van slachthuizen om te slachten volgens de israëlitische ritus: op verzoek van de Permanente Commissie tot de Algemene Zaken van het Nederlands-Israëlitisch Kerkgenootschap, en indien het betreft het aanwijzen van slachters om te slachten volgens de israëlitische ritus: op verzoek van het Opperrabbinaat voor Nederland;
b. indien het betreft het slachten volgens de islamitische ritus: op verzoek van de Commissie Islamitisch Slachten van het Contactorgaan Moslims en Overheid.

Artikel 3 (opleiding)
1. Ter uitvoering van het bepaalde in artikel 21 juncto bijlage IV, onderdeel g, van Verordening (EG) 1099/2009 met betrekking tot de opleiding voor personen in slachthuizen die handelingen verrichten die zien op het slachten volgens religieuze riten, worden na overleg met de convenants partijen nadere regels gesteld over opleidingen.
2. De opleidingen, bedoeld in het eerste lid, dienen in overeenstemming te zijn met de religieuze voorschriften betreffende de wijze van het slachten.

Artikel 4 (wetenschappelijke advies commissie voor onbedwelmd slachten volgens religieuze riten)
1. De convenantspartijen bepalen gezamenlijk welke onderzoeksvragen zij voor nadere wetenschappelijke advisering willen voorleggen.
2. De convenantspartijen bepalen per onderzoeksvraag welke wetenschapper(s) of instituten wordt gevraagd deze te beantwoorden.
3. De Staatssecretaris stelt na overleg met de overige convenantspartijen een wetenschappelijke adviescommissie in.
4. Convenantspartijen kunnen desgewenst een deskundige voordragen om plaats te laten nemen in de wetenschappelijke adviescommissie.
5. Op basis van de onderzoeksresultaten adviseert de wetenschappelijke adviescommissie aan de convenantspartijen.
[...]

Artikel 8 (inwerkingtreding)
Dit convenant treedt in werking één dag na ondertekening door alle convenantspartijen en wordt aangegaan voor onbepaalde tijd.

Jurisprudence

Case 1

Meat which does not result from ritual slaughter in accordance with the Islamic tradition (halal) can by no means be defined as halal, and the sale of such meat as halal meat is punishable. Despite the differences regarding the interpretation of halal within Islamic communities, in this case the Court referred to the commonly acknowledged definition, which is based on the general concept of ritual slaughter (i.e. slaughter conducted in accordance with the Islamic tradition). (Gerechtshof 's-Hertogenbosch, 2 May 2013, ECLI:NL:GHSHE:2013:BZ9218)[13]

Case 2

Ritual slaughtering of animals in accordance with religious (e.g. Islamic) tradition, i.e. with no prior stunning, can be conducted solely in accredited and registered slaughterhouses by properly qualified butchers. Moreover, slaughtering should be performed in conformity with the legal regulations and under control of the relevant authorities (with special attention being paid to food safety standards), primarily if the meat is to go to market. Cases of not conforming to the law are punished. (Rechtbank Midden-Nederland, 29 March 2013, ECLI:NL:RBMNE:2013:BZ7309)[14]

---

13 Available at http://uitspraken.rechtspraak.nl/inziendocument?id=ECLI:NL:GHSHE:2013:BZ9218 [last accessed on 12 February 2014].

14 Available at http://uitspraken.rechtspraak.nl/inziendocument?id=ECLI:NL:RBMNE:2013:BZ7309 [last accessed on 1 March 2014].

CHAPTER 12

Islamic Dress

When analysing the presence and manifestation of Islam in the Dutch public sphere, issues such as headscarves and the face veil are often raised. It should be noted that while Islamic headscarves have been accepted in the Dutch public sphere,[1] the practice of veiling faces causes much more controversy, triggering intense discussions. One of the frequently raised arguments is that a face veil considerably obscures the identification of an individual.[2] The character of the debate in this regard has also been influenced by direct references to the principle of religious freedom on the one hand, and state neutrality (i.e. also the neutrality of public premises and offices) on the other. The relatively

---

1 Nevertheless, one should note that in the course of public debate the postulation to forbid headscarves in the public sphere has regularly appeared. The radical right-wing party of Geert Wilders (*Groep Wilders*) presented this postulation in 2005. Two years later, the issue was raised again (in the same tone) by the right-wing Minister for Immigration, Rita Verdonk. These proposals have not been incorporated in relevant legal regulations, but they regularly appear in the discussion on face veils in the public sphere, especially as regards public schools. Sauer, 'Headscarf regimes in Europe …', p. 83. The motion was rejected, *inter alia* on the basis of its non-conformity with Art. 9 of the ECHR—see *Notitie van de Permanente Commissie van deskundigen in internationaal vreemdelingen-, vluchtelingen- en strafrecht naar aanleiding van de motie Wilders die een verbod van het openbaar gebruik van een boerka voorstaat*, Permanente Commissie van deskundigen in internationaal vreemdelingen-, vluchtelingen- en strafrecht, Utrecht 2006, available at http://www.commissie-meijers.nl/commissiemeijers/pagina.asp?pagkey=68551 [last accessed on 2 June 2014]. In 2012, a draft bill was issued, which was aimed to introduce a ban on face veiling. According to this proposal, the infringement of the ban would be fined. See *Instelling van een algemeen verbod op het dragen van gelaatsbedekkende kleding*, Tweede Kamer 2011–2012, 33165, no. 2, available at https://zoek.officielebekendmakingen.nl/dossier/33165/kst-33165-2?resultIndex=3&sorttype=1&sortorder=4 [last accessed on 25 July 2014]. See also the opinion of the Council of State: *Instelling van een algemeen verbod op het dragen van gelaatsbedekkende kleding*, Tweede Kamer 2011–2012, 33165, no. 4, available at https://zoek.officielebekendmakingen.nl/dossier/33165/kst-33165-4?resultIndex=6&sorttype=1&sortorder=4 [last accessed on 25 July 2014]. The draft was rejected by the Tweede Kamer. *Stemmingen lijst controversiële onderwerpen*, Tweede Kamer 2011/2012, no. 91, item 13, pp. 24–28, available at http://www.eerstekamer.nl/behandeling/20120605/stemming_in_verband_met/document3/f=/vjonmticonvr.pdf [last accessed on 30 June 2014].

2 It is worth noting that the Netherlands was the first European country where the face veil issue was politically discussed in Parliament.

heterogeneous character of Dutch society has triggered growing attention to the legal guarantees and protection of these tenets. One of the issues investigated by the CGB (followed by the CRM[3]) concerned Islamic dress, i.e. the right to manifest religious convictions in the public sphere through one's outfit, as well as the conditions and possible restrictions of religious freedom in this respect.

Aside from the Dutch Constitution, the AWGB is the primary source of the legal interpretation of the principles of equality and freedom in the Dutch system of law, also with regard to the manifestation of one's religious convictions and cultural identity. The AWGB broadly defines the principles of non-discrimination policy. Here one should stress the distinction between direct and indirect inequality, which has been defined in the AWGB, Art. 1c. This distinction plays a crucial role in the CGB's/CRM's adjudications. According to the law, direct inequality relates to differentiation deriving from one's religion, worldview or sex, and may be defined as a clear form of *discrimination*. Indirect inequality occurs in the situations where common and universal legal regulations, procedures and rules result in certain tensions of a religious, worldview, gender, racial etc. nature. Nevertheless, in this case, contrary to the *direct* distinction, such stipulations are not explicitly aimed at limiting one's freedom, and are both argued and justified e.g. by safety standards (e.g. uniforms in fire brigades and police forces).

The Dutch legislator does not forbid the presence of religious symbols or dress in the Dutch public sphere (public places, state premises). As aforementioned, such restrictions might nonetheless be introduced in particular cases (justified by the standards of state neutrality).[4] Dutch schools form an interesting case in this regard. Religiously-oriented schools (as examples of special schools) may introduce a ban on wearing certain religious symbols, on the basis of their right autonomously to define internal norms and rules (Art. 7c of the AWGB). At the same time, public schools are formally obliged to respect the principle of neutrality, although they are relatively free to interpret this rule in practice. After several court cases concerning bans on Islamic headscarves in schools, since 2003 (through a decision of the Ministry of Education) such regulations have become a school's internal issue and have been regulated within the boundaries of a school's authority. Schools have nevertheless been obliged to create detailed rules and guidelines on this matter,

3 See Chapter 11.

4 An interesting example of the adjudication and arguments used by the CGB with regard to court premises may be found e.g. in CGB 2001-53.

while more ambiguous cases have been delegated to the CGB/CRM.[5] It should also be noted that in many cases Islamic dress is an issue in employment law.[6]

The issues of Islamic dress are directly connected with the right to express one's religious convictions and manifest one's religious identity. Having said that, one should also refer to the legal interpretation of the Wom,[7] which directly refers to the public realm. According to Dutch law, in particular and legally defined cases (justified by safety requirements and the protection of public order) the freedom to wear religious dress may be limited.[8] The notion of 'the public' is defined in the Wom as the sphere which can be accessed with no limits by anyone. The aforementioned definition does not refer to places such as e.g. 'stadiums, post offices, warehouses, restaurants, museums, hospitals and churches'.[9] This list may be extended by court premises, public schools, state buildings and so forth. Any restrictions concerning the freedom to dress in accordance with one's religious beliefs may be applied in cases which fall beyond the scope of the aforepresented definition of the public sphere.

The ban on the face veil in Dutch state premises, schools and commercial institutions (such as banks or private enterprises), is usually argued on the basis of safety, communication and identification requirements. Moreover, the principles of the neutrality of state and public institutions are also taken into consideration. Nevertheless, in disputes concerning the freedom of employees in public offices, it is an employer who is obliged to prove that his work

5 Sauer, 'Headscarf regimes in Europe …', p. 82. Here, one should refer to the cases adjudicated on by the CGB, e.g. CGB 2011-2, available at http://mensenrechten.nl/publicaties/oordelen/2011-2 [last accessed on 15 January 2014] and CGB 2003-112, available at http://mensenrechten.nl/publicaties/oordelen/2003-112 [last accessed on 15 January 2014].

6 See Chapter 11. See also CGB 2006-248: a Muslim employee was not allowed to wear her headscarf in the shop where she worked, as the employer deemed it to be contraversion of the shop's image and dress code. The CGB concluded that indirect discrimination had occurred in this case. Available at http://mensenrechten.nl/publicaties/oordelen/2006-248 [last accessed on 27 January 2014].

7 See also Subchapter 1.2.

8 *Notitie van de Permanente Commissie* […] See also CGB 2003-40, available at http://mensenrechten.nl/publicaties/oordelen/2003-40 [last accessed on 15 January 2014]; CGB 2004-41, available at http://mensenrechten.nl/publicaties/oordelen/2004-41 [last accessed on 15 January 2014].

9 Tweede Kamer 1985–1986, 19427, no. 3, p. 15, available at http://resourcessgd.kb.nl/SGD/19851986/PDF/SGD_19851986_0007388.pdf [last accessed on 1 March 2014].

rules do not discriminate, and are both rationally and legally justified.[10] In the case of non-state institutions, an employer has more flexibility regarding the introduction of workplace clothing or behavioural principles.[11]

Algemene Wet Gelijke Behandeling

Artikel 1
1. In deze wet en de daarop berustende bepalingen wordt verstaan onder:
a. onderscheid: direct en indirect onderscheid, alsmede de opdracht daartoe;
b. direct onderscheid: indien een persoon op een andere wijze wordt behandeld dan een ander in een vergelijkbare situatie wordt, is of zou worden behandeld, op grond van godsdienst, levensovertuiging, politieke gezindheid, ras, geslacht, nationaliteit, hetero- of homoseksuele gerichtheid of burgerlijke staat;
c. indirect onderscheid: indien een ogenschijnlijk neutrale bepaling, maatstaf of handelwijze personen met een bepaalde godsdienst, levensovertuiging, politieke gezindheid, ras, geslacht, nationaliteit, hetero- of homoseksuele gerichtheid of burgerlijke staat in vergelijking met andere personen bijzonder treft.
2. Onder direct onderscheid op grond van geslacht wordt mede verstaan onderscheid op grond van zwangerschap, bevalling en moederschap.

Wet openbare manifestaties, 20 April 1988[12]

Artikel 1
1. In deze wet wordt verstaan onder openbare plaats: plaats die krachtens bestemming of vast gebruik openstaat voor het publiek.
2. Onder openbare plaats wordt niet begrepen een gebouw of besloten plaats als bedoeld in artikel 6, tweede lid, van de Grondwet.

10 See Vermeulen, Ben (ed.), *Overwegingen bij een boerka verbod. Zienswijze van de deskundigen inzake een verbod op gezichtsbedekkende kleding* (The Hague, 2006), p. 51, available at https://openaccess.leidenuniv.nl/bitstream/handle/1887/13377/7%20niqab_rapport.pdf?sequence=1 [last accessed on 24 February 2014].

11 Art. 9 of the ECHR primarily refers to the relations linking the state and its citizens. This document imposes on the state (also as an employer) the duty to protect the religious freedom of citizens. Private institutions benefit from a wider field of freedom in this matter. See Vermeulen (ed.), *Overwegingen bij een boerka verbod* …, p. 69.

12 Wet openbare manifestaties, available at http://wetten.overheid.nl/BWBR0004318 [last accessed on 2 June 2014].

Artikel 2
De bij of krachtens de bepalingen uit deze paragraaf aan overheidsorganen gegeven bevoegdheden tot beperking van het recht tot het belijden van godsdienst of levensovertuiging en het recht tot vergadering en betoging, kunnen slechts worden aangewend ter bescherming van de gezondheid, in het belang van het verkeer en ter bestrijding of voorkoming van wanordelijkheden.

Jurisprudence

Case 1

The ban on hiding one's face within the boundaries of a courtroom applies not only to court workers, but also e.g. to respondents and applicants. In this case, the Court refused a woman (respondent) the right to appear in court in a niqab. In the Court's adjudication, a ban on wearing a niqab during the judgement process was justified by the conditions of communication (e.g. body language). In the Court's opinion, the freedom of religion cannot override the principles and conditions of the Court's proceedings. The respondent, who refused to wear a headscarf instead of a niqab, was nevertheless allowed to be further represented by her lawyer. (Rechtbank Zwolle, 10 October 2003, ECLI:NL:RBZWO:2003:AL8382[13])

13 Available at http://uitspraken.rechtspraak.nl/inziendocument?id=ECLI:NL:RBZWO:2003:AL8382 [last accessed on 10 February 2014].

CHAPTER 13

Criminal Law

Dutch criminal law is encompassed by the Dutch Criminal Code (Wetboek van Strafrecht, hereafter WvSr), as amended, which originally dates back to 1881. The WvSr includes a number of provisions which either directly or indirectly refer to religious issues.

A range of articles included in the WvSr reveal state policy regarding religious freedom. As aforementioned, the WvSr was enacted at the end of the 19th century, a period marked by the considerably strong position and influence of Christian communities in the Netherlands. Nevertheless, the main principles and provisions included in the WvSr are of a relatively broad and universal character, and may equally be referred to Islam, e.g. with regard to the protection of Muslims against the acts of discrimination or blasphemy.[1]

The WvSr lists punishments that may be imposed in cases of infringing others' rights and freedoms. Art. 137c §1 of the WvSr assumes one year's imprisonment or a fine in the case of a deliberate (public, oral, written or pictographic) act offending others by reason of their race, religion, belief, sexual orientation or physical/mental disability. Cases of encouraging violence or hatred due to the features mentioned in Art. 137c and Art. 137d are also penalised, as well as 'support' for such acts. According to Art. 145, cases of violence interfering with a lawful assembly (including religious ceremonies and other forms of religious or ideological assemblies) are penalised as well. Legal protection against discrimination is particularly relevant during the conduct of professional functions, for instance in the administration and state posts (part II of the WvSr, Art. 429).

According to Art. 147 and Art. 147a of the WvSr, (public) blasphemy and behaviour aimed at offending someone's religious convictions and value system, are punishable.[2] The term 'God' should be understood here in a broad sense, i.e. it concerns all religious concepts of divine beings. This notion leads to further legal perplexities. Although this interpretation is relatively broad, as noted by A.L.J. Janssens and A.J. Nieuwenhuis, it does not encompass other

1 Janssens, Nieuwenhuis, *Uitingsdelicten*, p. 205.

2 The notion of the penalisation of blasphemous acts has been broadly discussed in the Dutch Parliament. The debate was additionally triggered by the motion submitted in 2013 by deputies Schouw (D66) and De Wit (SP) proposing the deletion of this provision from the WvSr. https://www.eerstekamer.nl/wetsvoorstel/32203_initiatiefvoorstel_schouw_en [last accessed on 2 January 2014].

objects of religious cult, e.g. the Virgin Mary, the saints and the prophets.[3] In Art. 147, three different aspects of blasphemy are emphasised: the broadly defined blasphemy in public, the legal protection of religious ministers, and the protection of religious objects (of worship).[4]

The aforementioned legal provisions of the WvSr focus on the public dimension of blasphemous utterances and activities. Nevertheless, it should be stressed that a ban on blasphemy does not involve a ban on expressing one's opinions on religious beliefs. Interestingly enough, a significant criterion in Dutch court judgments is one's *intentions* during the performance of blasphemous acts.[5] It is clear that such intentions are difficult to investigate or prove in practice. On the other hand, such notions allow for a broader interpretation of freedom to express one's convictions. It is worth noting that acts of public blasphemy may be penalised, even when no wounding of religious feelings is reported.[6] Additionally, in Dutch law the *context* is also taken into consideration, and plays a significant role in the qualification of one's behaviour in terms of blasphemy or offence. Dutch courts individually adjudicate on the cases, taking political and artistic aspects into account.[7]

The WvSr penalises acts of vandalism, desecration of corpses and cemeteries, as well as any forms of illegal activities concerning funerals (Articles 148–151). Besides this, the WvSr also envisages that a fine be imposed in cases when religious ministers conduct marriage in accordance with religious traditions before the civil marriage is concluded (Art. 449).[8]

Wetboek van Strafrecht, 3 March 1881[9]

Artikel 137c

1. Hij die zich in het openbaar, mondeling of bij geschrift of afbeelding, opzettelijk beledigend uitlaat over een groep mensen wegens hun ras, hun gods-

3 See a legal interpretation in: Janssens, Nieuwenhuis, *Uitingsdelicten*, p. 200. See also the case of Salman Rushdie's "The Satanic Verses"—according to Dutch law, this case could not be classified within the definition included in Art. 147 of the WvSr. Janssens, *Uitingsdelicten*, p. 260.

4 See Janssens, Nieuwenhuis, *Uitingsdelicten*, pp. 198–199.

5 Janssens, Nieuwenhuis, *Uitingsdelicten*, p. 201.

6 Janssens, Nieuwenhuis, *Uitingsdelicten*, p. 201.

7 See Nieuwenhuis, *Over de grens van …*, pp. 256–259 and Janssens, Nieuwenhuis, *Uitingsdelicten*, p. 203.

8 See Subchapter 15.2.

9 Wetboek van Strafrecht, available at http://wetten.overheid.nl/BWBR0001854 [last accessed on 2 January 2014].

dienst of levensovertuiging, hun hetero- of homoseksuele gerichtheid of hun lichamelijke, psychische of verstandelijke handicap, wordt gestraft met gevangenisstraf van ten hoogste een jaar of geldboete van de derde categorie.
2. Indien het feit wordt gepleegd door een persoon die daarvan een beroep of gewoonte maakt of door twee of meer verenigde personen wordt gevangenisstraf van ten hoogste twee jaren of geldboete van de vierde categorie opgelegd.

Artikel 137d
1. Hij die in het openbaar, mondeling of bij geschrift of afbeelding, aanzet tot haat tegen of discriminatie van mensen of gewelddadig optreden tegen persoon of goed van mensen wegens hun ras, hun godsdienst of levensovertuiging, hun geslacht, hun hetero- of homoseksuele gerichtheid of hun lichamelijke, psychische of verstandelijke handicap, wordt gestraft met gevangenisstraf van ten hoogste een jaar of geldboete van de derde categorie.
2. Indien het feit wordt gepleegd door een persoon die daarvan een beroep of gewoonte maakt of door twee of meer verenigde personen wordt gevangenisstraf van ten hoogste twee jaren of geldboete van de vierde categorie opgelegd.

Artikel 137e
1. Hij die, anders dan ten behoeve van zakelijke berichtgeving:
1°. een uitlating openbaar maakt die, naar hij weet of redelijkerwijs moet vermoeden, voor een groep mensen wegens hun ras, hun godsdienst of levensovertuiging, hun hetero- of homoseksuele gerichtheid of hun lichamelijke, psychische of verstandelijke handicap beledigend is, of aanzet tot haat tegen of discriminatie van mensen of gewelddadig optreden tegen persoon of goed van mensen wegens hun ras, hun godsdienst of levensovertuiging, hun geslacht, hun hetero- of homoseksuele gerichtheid of hun lichamelijke, psychische of verstandelijke handicap;
2°. een voorwerp waarin, naar hij weet of redelijkerwijs moet vermoeden, zulk een uitlating is vervat, aan iemand, anders dan op diens verzoek, doet toekomen, dan wel verspreidt of ter openbaarmaking van die uitlating of verspreiding in voorraad heeft; wordt gestraft met gevangenisstraf van ten hoogste zes maanden of geldboete van de derde categorie.
2. Indien het feit wordt gepleegd door een persoon die daarvan een beroep of gewoonte maakt of door twee of meer verenigde personen wordt gevangenisstraf van ten hoogste een jaar of geldboete van de vierde categorie opgelegd.

Artikel 137f
Hij die deelneemt of geldelijke of andere stoffelijke steun verleent aan activiteiten gericht op discriminatie van mensen wegens hun ras, hun gods-

dienst, hun levensovertuiging, hun geslacht, hun hetero- of homoseksuele gerichtheid of hun lichamelijke, psychische of verstandelijke handicap, wordt gestraft met gevangenisstraf van ten hoogste drie maanden of geldboete van de tweede categorie.
[...]

Artikel 145
Hij die door geweld of bedreiging met geweld hetzij een geoorloofde openbare samenkomst tot het belijden van godsdienst of levensovertuiging, hetzij een geoorloofde godsdienstige of levensbeschouwelijke plechtigheid of lijkplechtigheid verhindert, wordt gestraft met gevangenisstraf van ten hoogste een jaar of geldboete van de derde categorie.

Artikel 146
Hij die door het verwekken van wanorde of het maken van gedruis hetzij een geoorloofde openbare samenkomst tot het belijden van godsdienst of levensovertuiging, hetzij een geoorloofde godsdienstige of levensbeschouwelijke plechtigheid of lijkplechtigheid opzettelijk stoort, wordt gestraft met gevangenisstraf van ten hoogste twee maanden of geldboete van de tweede categorie.

Artikel 147
Met gevangenisstraf van ten hoogste drie maanden of geldboete van de tweede categorie wordt gestraft:
1°. hij die zich in het openbaar, mondeling of bij geschrift of afbeelding, door smalende godslasteringen op voor godsdienstige gevoelens krenkende wijze uitlaat;
2°. hij die een bedienaar van de godsdienst in de geoorloofde waarneming van zijn bediening bespot;
3°. hij die voorwerpen aan een eredienst gewijd, waar en wanneer de uitoefening van die dienst geoorloofd is, beschimpt.

Artikel 147a
1. Hij die een geschrift of afbeelding waarin uitlatingen voorkomen die, als smalende godslasteringen, voor godsdienstige gevoelens krenkend zijn, verspreidt, openlijk tentoonstelt of aanslaat of, om verspreid, openlijk tentoongesteld of aangeslagen te worden, in voorraad heeft, wordt, indien hij weet of ernstige reden heeft om te vermoeden dat in het geschrift of de afbeelding zodanige uitlatingen voorkomen, gestraft met gevangenisstraf van ten hoogste twee maanden of geldboete van de tweede categorie.

2. Met dezelfde straf wordt gestraft hij die, met gelijke wetenschap of een gelijke reden tot vermoeden, de inhoud van een zodanig geschrift openlijk ten gehore brengt.

Artikel 148
Hij die opzettelijk de geoorloofde toegang tot een begraafplaats of crematorium of het geoorloofd vervoer van een lijk naar een begraafplaats of crematorium verhindert of belemmert, wordt gestraft met gevangenisstraf van ten hoogste een maand of geldboete van de tweede categorie.

Artikel 149
Hij die opzettelijk een graf schendt of enig op een begraafplaats opgericht gedenkteken opzettelijk en wederrechtelijk vernielt of beschadigt, wordt gestraft met gevangenisstraf van ten hoogste een jaar of geldboete van de derde categorie.

Artikel 150
Hij die opzettelijk en wederrechtelijk een lijk opgraaft of wegneemt of een opgegraven of weggenomen lijk verplaatst of vervoert, wordt gestraft met gevangenisstraf van ten hoogste een jaar of geldboete van de derde categorie.

Artikel 151
Hij die een lijk begraaft, verbrandt, vernietigt, verbergt, wegvoert of wegmaakt, met het oogmerk om het feit of de oorzaak van het overlijden, dan wel van het dood ter wereld komen te verhelen, wordt gestraft met gevangenisstraf van ten hoogste twee jaren of geldboete van de vierde categorie.
[...]

Artikel 429bis
Hij die op een van de openbare weg zichtbare plaats woorden of afbeeldingen stelt of gesteld houdt, die, als smalende godslasteringen, voor godsdienstige gevoelens krenkend zijn, wordt gestraft met hechtenis van ten hoogste een maand of geldboete van de tweede categorie.
[...]

Artikel 429quater
1. Hij die in de uitoefening van een ambt, beroep of bedrijf personen discrimineert wegens hun ras, hun godsdienst, hun levensovertuiging, hun geslacht of hun hetero- of homoseksuele gerichtheid wordt gestraft met hechtenis van ten hoogste twee maanden of geldboete van de derde categorie.

2. Met dezelfde straf wordt gestraft hij wiens handelen of nalaten in de uitoefening van een ambt, beroep of bedrijf zonder redelijke grond, ten doel heeft of ten gevolge kan hebben dat ten aanzien van personen met een lichamelijke, psychische of verstandelijke handicap de erkenning, het genot of de uitoefening op voet van gelijkheid van de rechten van de mens en de fundamentele vrijheden op politiek, economisch, sociaal of cultureel terrein of op andere terreinen van het maatschappelijk leven, wordt teniet gedaan of aangetast.
[...]

Artikel 449
1. De bedienaar van de godsdienst die, voordat partijen hem hebben doen blijken dat hun huwelijk ten overstaan van de ambtenaar van de burgerlijke stand is voltrokken, enige godsdienstige plechtigheid daartoe betrekkelijk verricht, wordt gestraft met geldboete van de tweede categorie.

Jurisprudence

Case 1

In the case of Geert Wilders, a Dutch radical right-wing politician, the Court investigated his negative statements regarding the culture of Islam, including the Qur'an (which was e.g. compared to Hitler's *Mein Kampf*). The respondent's statements were expressed in the course of public debate, both orally and in writing (e.g. in the press and on the Internet), as well as in other audiovisual forms (the film 'Fitna'). The Court argued that critical, even offensive, opinions regarding religious convictions could not be automatically penalised on the grounds that their followers felt offended thereby. In other words, such critical statements concerning religion and particular religious convictions and beliefs cannot be automatically equated with statements which directly target their followers. In the Court's opinion, the investigated views encompassed Islam and Islamic culture but they did not target Muslims *per se*. Moreover, the Court referred to the legal argument that the conditions of public debate require special consideration of the freedom of expression. The Court acquitted the respondent of the charges, i.e. 1) expressing insulting statements concerning a group of people due to their religious conviction, 2) incitement to hatred against Muslims, and 3) incitement of the discrimination of Muslims due to their religious convictions. (Rechtbank Amsterdam, 23 June 2011, ECLI:NL:RBAMS:2011:BQ9001)[10]

10 Available at http://uitspraken.rechtspraak.nl/inziendocument?id=ECLI:NL:RBAMS:2011:

Case 2

The Court referred to the legal reasoning offered by the Public Prosecutor. A statement or expressed view can be penalised only on the grounds of its objectively discriminatory character. Nevertheless, objectively discriminatory statements are not penalised if they are expressed in the course of a social (public) debate, which allows for 'shocking, sharp or offensive' utterances. (Parket bij de Hoge Raad, 10 March 2009, ECLI:NL:PHR:2009:BF0655)[11]

BQ9001 [last accessed on 7 February 2014]. See also the case regarding the legal interpretation of Art. 137c of the WvSr—Hoge Raad, 10 March 2009, ECLI:NL:HR:2009:BF0655, available at http://uitspraken.rechtspraak.nl/inziendocument?id=ECLI:NL:HR:2009:BF0655 [last accessed on 8 February 2014].

11 Available at http://uitspraken.rechtspraak.nl/inziendocument?id=ECLI:NL:PHR:2009:BF0655 [last accessed on 1 March 2014].

CHAPTER 14

Family Law

14.1 Private International Law

By 2012 private international law (*internationaal privaatrecht*) issues had been regulated by a number of legal acts. Since 1 January 2012 private international law matters have been encompassed by the BW, Book 10.[1] The main aim of this legislative development was to allow for the thorough inclusion of varied aspects of private international law in one legal Act.

According to Art. 3 of the BW, Book 10, Dutch law shall be applied as the primary legislative principle (*lex fori*). Foreign legal rules cannot be applied if they do not conform to Dutch legal order.[2]

Burgerlijk Wetboek Boek 10, Internationaal Privaatrecht[3]

Artikel 1
De in dit Boek en andere wettelijke regelingen vervatte regels van internationaal privaatrecht laten de werking van voor Nederland bindende internationale en communautaire regelingen onverlet.

Artikel 2
De regels van internationaal privaatrecht en het door die regels aangewezen recht worden ambtshalve toegepast.

Artikel 3
Op de wijze van procederen ten overstaan van de Nederlandse rechter is het Nederlandse recht van toepassing.

1 See also the report concerning the consolidation of legal acts on private international law: *Algemene bepalingen Wet internationaal privaatrecht*, Rapport aan de Minister van Justitie, Staatscommissie voor het internationaal privaatrecht, 's Gravenhage, 1 June 2002, available at http://www.rijksoverheid.nl/bestanden/documenten-en-publicaties/rapporten/2002/06/01/rapport-algemene-bepalingen-ipr/rapportalgemenebepalingenipr.pdf [last accessed on 25 January 2014].

2 See also Chapter 16.2. See Berger, Maurits, 'Sharia in Nederland is vaak keurig Nederlands', *Mens en Maatschappij*, no. 56 (2007), pp. 506–510.

3 Burgerlijk Wetboek Boek 10, Internationaal Privaatrecht, available at http://wetten.overheid.nl/BWBR0030068 [last accessed on 25 January 2014].

Artikel 4
Indien de vraag welke rechtsgevolgen aan een feit toekomen bij wijze van voorvraag in verband met een andere, aan vreemd recht onderworpen vraag moet worden beantwoord, wordt de voorvraag beschouwd als een zelfstandige vraag.

Artikel 5
Onder de toepassing van het recht van een staat wordt verstaan de toepassing van de rechtsregels die in die staat gelden met uitzondering van het internationaal privaatrecht.

Artikel 6
Vreemd recht wordt niet toegepast, voor zover de toepassing ervan kennelijk onverenigbaar is met de openbare orde.

Artikel 7
1. Bepalingen van bijzonder dwingend recht zijn bepalingen aan de inachtneming waarvan een staat zo veel belang hecht voor de handhaving van zijn openbare belangen, zoals zijn politieke, sociale of economische organisatie, dat zij moeten worden toegepast op elk geval dat onder de werkingssfeer ervan valt, ongeacht welk recht overigens van toepassing is.
2. De toepassing van het recht waarnaar een verwijzingsregel verwijst, blijft achterwege, voor zover in het gegeven geval bepalingen van Nederlands bijzonder dwingend recht toepasselijk zijn. 3. Bij de toepassing van het recht waarnaar een verwijzingsregel verwijst, kan gevolg worden toegekend aan bepalingen van bijzonder dwingend recht van een vreemde staat waarmee het geval nauw is verbonden. Bij de beslissing of aan deze bepalingen gevolg moet worden toegekend, wordt rekening gehouden met hun aard en strekking alsmede met de gevolgen die uit het toepassen of het niet toepassen van deze bepalingen zouden voortvloeien.
[...]

Artikel 11
1. Of een natuurlijke persoon minderjarig is en in hoeverre hij bekwaam is rechtshandelingen te verrichten, wordt bepaald door zijn nationale recht. Indien de betrokken persoon de nationaliteit van meer dan een staat bezit en hij in een van deze staten zijn gewone verblijfplaats heeft, geldt het recht van die staat als zijn nationale recht. Heeft hij zijn gewone verblijfplaats niet in een van deze staten, dan geldt als zijn nationale recht het recht van de staat van zijn nationaliteit, waarmee hij alle omstandigheden in aanmerking genomen het nauwst verbonden is.

2. Ten aanzien van een meerzijdige rechtshandeling die valt buiten het toepassingsgebied van de Verordening (EG) Nr. 593/2008 van het Europees Parlement en de Raad van 17 juni 2008 inzake het recht dat van toepassing is op verbintenissen uit overeenkomst (Rome I) (PbEU L 177) is artikel 13 van die Verordening van overeenkomstige toepassing op het beroep op handelingsonbekwaamheid of handelingsonbevoegdheid van een natuurlijk persoon die partij is bij die rechtshandeling.

14.2 Marriage and Divorce

On 1 January 2012, the Act on Conflicts regarding the Dissolution of Marriage and Separation from Bed and Board (Wet conflictenrecht inzake ontbinding huwelijk en scheiding van tafel en bed) of 1981 and the Act on Marriage Conflicts of Laws (Wet Conflictenrecht Huwelijk) of 1989 were repealed. The provisions concerning marriage and marital status issues were included in the BW, Book 10.[4]

In the Netherlands, a civil marriage must be conducted before a religious marriage, as the latter form *per se* has no effect in civil law.[5] This principle is explicitly stated in Art. 67 and Art. 68 of the BW, Book 1. According to Art. 68, no religious ceremony may take place prior to a civil marriage. Moreover, the WvSr envisages in Art. 449 a fine for officials who infringe this rule.[6] Additionally, the conditions of divorce, the end of marriage, the dissolution and its potential transformation (e.g. into the form of a cohabitation agreement) are clearly set out in Articles 149–154 of the BW, Book 1.

One of the issues in Dutch family law which may indirectly form the point of reference to the situation of Muslims in the Netherlands is the nationality of (intended) spouses. Interestingly enough, in several decisions of the Dutch courts the distinction between 'nationality' and 'domicile' formed the legal point of reference for adjudication in cases where the parties (i.e. a couple) invoked (or could invoke) different national laws.[7] Court references to the principle of domicile allow for the application of Dutch law on the basis of

4 See Chapter 16.1.

5 See Potz, Wieshaider, 'Religious Entities as Legal Persons …', p. 34.

6 See Chapter 14.

7 Regarding the so-called 'better law approach' see Foblets, Marie-Claire, Overbeeke, Adriaan, 'Islam in Belgium' in *Islam and the European Union*, Potz, Richard, Wieshaider, Wolfgang (eds.) (Leuven: Peeters, 2004), p. 29.

parties bound to Dutch culture, and thereby also to the Dutch system of law.[8] Moreover, it should be stressed that an increasing number of Muslims have Dutch nationality, which forms the foundation for the application of Dutch national law.[9]

Particular religious principles and traditions may lead to certain perplexities in the interpretation of Dutch family law. Regarding the issues of marriage and divorce, one should consider matters such as a requirement to marry a Muslim, the position of women and their rights, arranged marriages or polygamy (e.g. in the case of Moroccan marriages). These issues have not been directly referred to in the Dutch system of law; however they have been subject to legal interpretations and numerous court adjudications.

One of the issues discussed regarding private international law concerns the recognition of repudation in the Netherlands. Here, one should refer to Art. 58 of the BW, Book 10, which states that the unilateral dissolution of marriage, conducted abroad, can be recognised in the Netherlands provided that the listed conditions are met, i.e. the dissolution conforms to the national law of a spouse's country of origin, has legal consequences in that country, and the other spouse either explicitly or implicitly agrees to dissolve the marriage.

Dutch law states that marriage is defined as the legal relation of two persons, thereby forbidding bigamy and polygamy.[10] The legislator however envisages the form of a cohabitation agreement (*samenlevingsovereenkomst*) which leaves more room for both the form of such a relationship, including the reference to religious traditions such as polygamy,[11] and the rules of repudation.

Burgerlijk Wetboek Boek 1, Personen- en familierecht[12]

Artikel 30

1. Een huwelijk kan worden aangegaan door twee personen van verschillend of van gelijk geslacht.

8 Foblets, Overbeeke, 'Islam in Belgium', p. 29.

9 See Berger, 'Sharia in Nederland ...', p. 507.

10 Nevertheless, a polygamous marriage which was conducted abroad, in accordance with the respective state law, can be recognised in the Netherlands. Regarding legal interpretation see more in Boer, Jan de, *Personen- en familierecht* (Deventer: Kluwer 2010), 8th edition, pp. 139–140.

11 Regarding a cohabitation agreement between three persons see https://zoek.officielebekendmakingen.nl/kv-20050600330.html [last accessed on 10 January 2014].

12 Burgerlijk Wetboek Boek 1, Personen- en familierecht, available at http://www.wetboek-online.nl/wet/Burgerlijk%20Wetboek%20Boek%201.html#322 [last accessed on 1 January 2014].

2. De wet beschouwt het huwelijk alleen in zijn burgerlijke betrekkingen.

Artikel 31
1. Om een huwelijk te mogen aangaan moeten een man en een vrouw de leeftijd van achttien jaren hebben bereikt.
2. Het in het vorige lid vermelde huwelijksbeletsel bestaat niet wanneer zij die met elkander een huwelijk willen aangaan de leeftijd van zestien jaren hebben bereikt en de vrouw een verklaring van een arts overlegt dat zij zwanger is, dan wel haar kind reeds ter wereld heeft gebracht.
3. Onze Minister van Justitie kan om gewichtige redenen ontheffing verlenen van het in het eerste lid genoemde vereiste.

Artikel 32
Een huwelijk mag niet worden aangegaan, wanneer de geestvermogens van een partij zodanig zijn gestoord, dat deze niet in staat is haar wil te bepalen of de betekenis van haar verklaring te begrijpen.

Artikel 33
Een persoon kan tegelijkertijd slechts met één andere persoon door het huwelijk verbonden zijn.
[...]

Artikel 35
1. Een minderjarige mag geen huwelijk aangaan zonder toestemming van zijn ouders.
2. Zijn de geestvermogens van een ouder zodanig gestoord, dat hij niet in staat is zijn wil te bepalen of de betekenis van zijn verklaring te begrijpen, dan is zijn toestemming niet vereist.
3. Een minderjarige, die onder voogdij staat, heeft bovendien de toestemming van zijn voogd nodig.

Artikel 36
Voor zover een volgens het vorige artikel vereiste toestemming niet wordt verkregen, kan zij op verzoek van de minderjarige door die van de rechtbank worden vervangen.
[...]

Artikel 41
1. Een huwelijk mag niet worden gesloten tussen hen die elkander, hetzij van nature hetzij familierechtelijk, bestaan in de opgaande en in de nederdalende lijn of als broeders, zusters of broeder en zuster.

2. Onze Minister van Justitie kan om gewichtige redenen ontheffing van het verbod verlenen aan hen die broeders, zusters of broeder en zuster door adoptie zijn.

Artikel 42
Zij die met elkander een huwelijk willen aangaan, mogen niet tegelijkertijd een geregistreerd partnerschap zijn aangegaan.
[...]

Artikel 65
De aanstaande echtgenoten zijn verplicht bij de voltrekking van hun huwelijk in persoon voor de ambtenaar van de burgerlijke stand te verschijnen.

Artikel 66
Het staat Onze Minister van Justitie vrij, uit hoofde van gewichtige redenen aan partijen te vergunnen het huwelijk door een bijzondere bij authentieke akte gevolmachtigde te voltrekken.

Artikel 67
1. De aanstaande echtgenoten moeten ten overstaan van de ambtenaar van de burgerlijke stand en in tegenwoordigheid van de getuigen verklaren, dat zij elkander aannemen tot echtgenoten en dat zij getrouw alle plichten zullen vervullen, die door de wet aan de huwelijkse staat worden verbonden.
2. Terstond nadat deze verklaring is afgelegd, verklaart de ambtenaar van de burgerlijke stand, dat partijen door de echt aan elkander zijn verbonden, en maakt hij daarvan in het daartoe bestemde register een akte op.

Artikel 68
Geen godsdienstige plechtigheden zullen mogen plaats hebben, voordat de partijen aan de bedienaar van de eredienst zullen hebben doen blijken, dat het huwelijk ten overstaan van de ambtenaar van de burgerlijke stand is voltrokken.

Artikel 69
1. Voor zover hieronder niet anders is bepaald, kan op grond dat de echtgenoten niet de vereisten in zich verenigden om tezamen een huwelijk aan te gaan, de nietigverklaring van het huwelijk worden verzocht door:
a de bloedverwanten in de opgaande lijn van een der echtgenoten;
b ieder der echtgenoten;
c alle overige personen, die daarbij een onmiddellijk rechtsbelang hebben, echter deze alleen na de ontbinding van het huwelijk;

d het openbaar ministerie, echter alleen zolang het huwelijk niet is ontbonden.
2. Hij die met een der echtgenoten nog door een vroeger huwelijk dan wel door een eerder geregistreerd partnerschap is verbonden, is eveneens bevoegd op grond van het bestaan van dat huwelijk of die registratie de nietigverklaring van het daarna gesloten huwelijk te verzoeken.

Artikel 70
1. Op verzoek van de ouders, de echtgenoten en het openbaar ministerie kan een huwelijk worden nietig verklaard, wanneer het ten overstaan van een niet bevoegde ambtenaar van de burgerlijke stand of niet in tegenwoordigheid van het vereiste aantal getuigen is voltrokken.
2. De bevoegdheid van een echtgenoot om uit dien hoofde de nietigverklaring van het huwelijk te verzoeken vervalt, indien er uiterlijk bezit van de huwelijkse staat en een akte van huwelijksvoltrekking ten overstaan van een ambtenaar van de burgerlijke stand verleden, aanwezig zijn.

Artikel 71
1. Een echtgenoot kan de nietigverklaring van zijn huwelijk verzoeken, wanneer dit onder invloed van een onrechtmatige ernstige bedreiging is gesloten.
2. Een gelijk verzoek komt de echtgenoot toe, die bij de huwelijksvoltrekking gedwaald heeft hetzij in de persoon van de andere echtgenoot, hetzij omtrent de betekenis van de door hem afgelegde verklaring.
3. De bevoegdheid van de echtgenoot de nietigverklaring wegens bedreiging of dwaling te verzoeken vervalt, wanneer de echtgenoten zes maanden hebben samengewoond sedert het ophouden van de bedreiging of de ontdekking van de dwaling, zonder dat het verzoek is gedaan.

Artikel 71a
Op verzoek van het openbaar ministerie kan een huwelijk als schijnhandeling wegens strijd met de Nederlandse openbare orde worden nietig verklaard indien het oogmerk van de echtgenoten, of één hunner, niet was gericht op de vervulling van de door de wet aan de huwelijkse staat verbonden plichten, doch op het verkrijgen van toelating tot Nederland.
[...]

Artikel 149
Het huwelijk eindigt:
a door de dood;
b indien de vermiste, die overeenkomstig de bepalingen van de tweede of derde afdeling van de achttiende titel van dit boek vermoedelijk overleden

dan wel overleden is verklaard, nog in leven is op de dag waarop de achtergebleven echtgenoot een nieuw huwelijk of geregistreerd partnerschap is aangegaan: door de voltrekking van dit huwelijk of geregistreerd partnerschap;
c door echtscheiding, overeenkomstig de bepalingen van de tweede afdeling van deze titel;
d door ontbinding van het huwelijk na scheiding van tafel en bed, overeenkomstig de bepalingen van de tweede afdeling van de tiende titel van dit boek;
e door omzetting van een huwelijk in een geregistreerd partnerschap.

Afdeling 2. Echtscheiding

Artikel 150
Echtscheiding tussen echtgenoten die niet van tafel en bed gescheiden zijn, wordt uitgesproken op verzoek van één der echtgenoten of op hun gemeenschappelijk verzoek.

Artikel 151
Echtscheiding wordt op verzoek van één der echtgenoten uitgesproken, indien het huwelijk duurzaam ontwricht is.
[...]

Artikel 154
1. Echtscheiding wordt op gemeenschappelijk verzoek van de echtgenoten uitgesproken indien het verzoek is gegrond op hun beider oordeel dat het huwelijk duurzaam ontwricht is.
2. Ieder der echtgenoten is tot op het tijdstip der uitspraak bevoegd het verzoek in te trekken.

Burgerlijk Wetboek Boek 10, Internationaal Privaatrecht[13]

Artikel 55
Ontbinding van het huwelijk en scheiding van tafel en bed kunnen in Nederland uitsluitend worden uitgesproken door de Nederlandse rechter.

---

13 Burgerlijk Wetboek Boek 10, Internationaal Privaatrecht, available at http://wetten.overheid.nl/BWBR0030068 [last accessed on 25 January 2014].

Artikel 56
1. Of ontbinding van het huwelijk of scheiding van tafel en bed kan worden uitgesproken en op welke gronden, wordt bepaald door het Nederlandse recht.
2. In afwijking van lid 1 wordt het recht van de staat van een gemeenschappelijke vreemde nationaliteit van de echtgenoten toegepast indien in het geding:
a. door de echtgenoten gezamenlijk een keuze voor dit recht is gedaan of een dergelijke keuze van een van de echtgenoten onweersproken is gebleven; of
b. door een van de echtgenoten een keuze voor dit recht is gedaan en beide echtgenoten een werkelijke maatschappelijke band met het land van die gemeenschappelijke nationaliteit hebben.
3. Een rechtskeuze als bedoeld in het vorige lid moet uitdrukkelijk zijn gedaan of anderszins voldoende duidelijk blijken uit de in het verzoekschrift of het verweerschrift gebruikte bewoordingen.

Artikel 57
1. Een in het buitenland na een behoorlijke rechtspleging verkregen ontbinding van het huwelijk of scheiding van tafel en bed wordt in Nederland erkend, indien zij is tot stand gekomen door de beslissing van een rechter of andere autoriteit en indien aan die rechter of andere autoriteit daartoe rechtsmacht toekwam.
2. Een in het buitenland verkregen ontbinding van het huwelijk of scheiding van tafel en bed die niet voldoet aan één of meer van de in lid 1 gestelde voorwaarden wordt nochtans in Nederland erkend, indien duidelijk blijkt dat de wederpartij hetzij tijdens de buitenlandse procedure uitdrukkelijk of stilzwijgend met die ontbinding of scheiding van tafel en bed heeft ingestemd, dan wel na afloop van de procedure in de uitspraak heeft berust.

Artikel 58
Een ontbinding van het huwelijk in het buitenland die uitsluitend door een eenzijdige verklaring van een der echtgenoten is tot stand gekomen, wordt erkend indien:
a. de ontbinding in deze vorm overeenstemt met een nationaal recht van de echtgenoot, die het huwelijk eenzijdig heeft ontbonden;
b. de ontbinding in de staat waar zij geschiedde rechtsgevolg heeft; en
c. duidelijk blijkt dat de andere echtgenoot uitdrukkelijk of stilzwijgend met de ontbinding heeft ingestemd dan wel daarin heeft berust.

Artikel 59
Ongeacht de artikelen 57 en 58 van dit Boek wordt aan een in het buitenland tot stand gekomen ontbinding van het huwelijk erkenning onthouden indien deze erkenning kennelijk onverenigbaar is met de openbare orde.

Jurisprudence

Case 1

A Pakistani couple married via the telephone in the presence of an imam and witnesses on both sides, in accordance with the Pakistani law. The marriage certificate was recognised by the Dutch state and registered in the respective municipal register in the Netherlands. (Rechtbank 's-Gravenhage, 10 March 2008, ECLI:NL:RBSGR:2008:BC6188)[14]

Case 2

An Egyptian respondent sought to annul his marriage in the Netherlands having already divorced. The respondent argued that due to the bigamous character of his marital status, after divorcing his first wife the marriage should be annulled according to Dutch law, i.e. on the grounds of a legal ban on bigamy and polygamy. The marriage was conducted in Egypt, the country of origin of both ex-spouses, who were both also Muslims. According to Egyptian law and Islamic tradition, the act of marriage cannot be annulled based on its bigamous character, which is legal in Egypt. Moreover, the respondents were of Egyptian, not Dutch, nationality. According to the Court, in this case both Egyptian law and Islamic principles should be referred to. Therefore, in the Court's opinion, Dutch law could not be applied and the marriage could not be annulled in the Netherlands. (Rechtbank Den Haag, 22 May 2013, ECLI:NL:RBDHA:2013:CA2361)[15]

Case 3

A man sought the recognition of the dissolution of his marriage through the procedure of repudation, which was conducted in Morocco in accordance with Moroccan law. The man was refused by municipal authorities to have this repudation legally recognised through registration. The Court upheld this decision and argument, and held that the repudation could not be recognised

14 Available at http://uitspraken.rechtspraak.nl/inziendocument?id=ECLI:NL:RBSGR:2008:BC6188 [last accessed on 11 February 2014].

15 Available at http://uitspraken.rechtspraak.nl/inziendocument?id=ECLI:NL:RBDHA:2013:CA2361 [last accessed on 25 February 2014].

in the Netherlands on the grounds that the marriage was not dissolved by the proper legal authorities. Besides this, the will of the respondent's wife was not explicitly expressed. (Raad van State, 3 March 2010, ECLI:NL:RVS:2010:BL6235)[16]

14.3 Children

Legal issues concerning children (parentage, adoption, minors, parental authority, legal guardians, the costs of maintenance and education) are included in the BW, Book 1 (Articles 197–408). Issues concerning parental authority are defined in Art. 251 and Art. 253. According to Dutch law, in the event of the parents' divorce, parental authority is subject to the court's decision. The law also adjudicates on cases of automatic marital authority under certain conditions (Art. 253b)—the court is also the competent body for such decisions. With reference to the education and upbringing of children, Dutch law leaves much space for parents' autonomy.[17] This principle also concerns religious practices and traditions, such as male circumcision of a minor. However, in cases of the infringement of children's rights and freedoms, the Dutch legislator envisages the opportunity for the state's interference.

Burgerlijk Wetboek Boek 1 Personen- en familierecht[18]

Artikel 251
1. Gedurende hun huwelijk oefenen de ouders het gezag gezamenlijk uit.
2. Na ontbinding van het huwelijk anders dan door de dood of na scheiding van tafel en bed blijven de ouders die gezamenlijk het gezag hebben, dit gezag gezamenlijk uitoefenen, tenzij de rechter op verzoek van de ouders of een van hen in het belang van het kind bepaalt dat het gezag over een kind of de kinderen aan een van hen alleen toekomt.
3. De beslissing op grond van het tweede lid wordt gegeven bij de beschikking houdende scheiding van tafel en bed, echtscheiding dan wel ontbinding van het huwelijk na scheiding van tafel en bed of bij latere beschikking. Totdat het gezag van één van beide ouders aanvangt, komt dit toe aan degene die ook

16 Available at http://uitspraken.rechtspraak.nl/inziendocument?id=ECLI:NL:RVS:2010:BL6235 [last accessed on 1 January 2014].

17 See Loenen, *Geloof in het geding* ..., pp. 47–48.

18 Burgerlijk Wetboek Boek 1 Personen- en familierecht, available at http://www.wetboek-online.nl/wet/Burgerlijk%20Wetboek%20Boek%201.html#322 [last accessed on 1 January 2014].

tijdens het geding het gezag uitoefende, zulks met dezelfde bevoegdheden en onder dezelfde verplichtingen als deze toen had.
4. Indien een beslissing op grond van het tweede lid niet alle kinderen der echtgenoten betrof, vult de rechtbank haar aan op verzoek van een der ouders, van de raad voor de kinderbescherming of ambtshalve.

Artikel 251a
De rechter kan, indien hem blijkt dat de minderjarige van twaalf jaar of ouder hierop prijs stelt, ambtshalve een beslissing geven op de voet van artikel 251, tweede lid. Hetzelfde geldt indien de minderjarige de leeftijd van twaalf jaren nog niet heeft bereikt, maar in staat kan worden geacht tot een redelijke waardering van zijn belangen ter zake.

Artikel 252
1. De ouders die niet met elkaar zijn gehuwd noch met elkaar gehuwd zijn geweest en die nimmer het gezag over hun minderjarige kinderen gezamenlijk hebben uitgeoefend, oefenen dit gezamenlijk uit, indien zulks op hun beider verzoek in het in artikel 244 van dit boek bedoelde register is aangetekend.
2. De aantekening wordt door de griffier geweigerd, indien op het tijdstip van het verzoek:
a) één of beide ouders onbevoegd is tot het gezag; of
b) één van beide ouders is ontheven of ontzet van het gezag en de andere ouder het gezag uitoefent; of
c) een voogd met het gezag over het kind is belast; of
d) de voorziening in het gezag over het kind is komen te ontbreken; of
e) de ouder die het gezag heeft, dit gezamenlijk met een ander dan een ouder uitoefent.
3. Tegen de weigering van de aantekening is alleen beroep mogelijk, indien zij heeft plaatsgevonden op grond van onbevoegdheid van één of beide ouders tot het gezag anders dan vanwege minderjarigheid of ondercuratelestelling. Alsdan kan de rechtbank worden verzocht de aantekening te gelasten. Zij wijst het verzoek af, indien gegronde vrees bestaat dat bij inwilliging de belangen van het kind zouden worden verwaarloosd.

Artikel 253
1. Indien gewezen echtgenoten met elkaar hertrouwen dan wel een geregistreerd partnerschap aangegaan en onmiddellijk daaraan voorafgaande één der echtgenoten het gezag over de minderjarige kinderen uitoefende, herleeft van rechtswege het gezamenlijk gezag, tenzij een der echtgenoten onbevoegd

is tot dit gezag of daarvan is ontheven of ontzet dan wel het gezag gezamenlijk met een ander dan de ouder uitoefent.
2. De echtgenoot voor wie het gezag niet is herleefd, kan de rechtbank verzoeken hem daarmede te belasten. Dit verzoek wordt slechts afgewezen, indien gegronde vrees bestaat dat bij inwilliging de belangen van de kinderen zouden worden verwaarloosd.
3. Het eerste en tweede lid zijn van overeenkomstige toepassing, indien door verzoening van de echtgenoten een scheiding van tafel en bed eindigt.
4. Het eerste en tweede lid zijn van overeenkomstige toepassing indien gewezen geregistreerde partners die gezamenlijk gezag uitoefenden over het kind, opnieuw met elkaar een geregistreerd partnerschap aangaan dan wel met elkaar huwen.

Artikel 253a
Ingeval van gezamenlijke gezagsuitoefening kunnen geschillen tussen de ouders hieromtrent op verzoek van beiden of van een van hen aan de rechtbank worden voorgelegd. Deze beproeft, alvorens te beslissen, een vergelijk tussen de ouders. De rechtbank neemt een zodanige beslissing als haar in het belang van het kind wenselijk voorkomt.

Artikel 253aa
1. Over een staande een geregistreerd partnerschap geboren kind oefenen de ouders gezamenlijk het gezag uit.
2. De bepalingen met betrekking tot het gezamenlijk gezag van ouders zijn hierop van toepassing, met uitzondering van de artikelen 251, tweede, derde en vierde lid, en 251a.

Artikel 253b
1. Indien ten aanzien van een kind alleen het moederschap vaststaat of indien de ouders van een kind niet met elkaar gehuwd zijn dan wel gehuwd zijn geweest en zij het gezag niet gezamenlijk uitoefenen, oefent de moeder van rechtswege het gezag over het kind alleen uit, tenzij zij bij haar bevalling onbevoegd tot het gezag was.
2. De in het eerste lid bedoelde moeder die ten tijde van haar bevalling onbevoegd was tot het gezag, verkrijgt dit van rechtswege op het tijdstip waarop zij daartoe bevoegd wordt, tenzij op dat tijdstip een ander met het gezag is belast.
3. Indien op bedoeld tijdstip een ander het gezag heeft, kan de tot het gezag bevoegde ouder de rechtbank verzoeken hem met het gezag over het kind te belasten.

4. Wanneer de andere ouder het gezag over het kind uitoefent, wordt dit verzoek slechts ingewilligd, indien de rechter dit in het belang van het kind wenselijk oordeelt.
5. Wanneer een voogd het gezag over het kind uitoefent, wordt het verzoek slechts afgewezen, indien gegronde vrees bestaat dat bij inwilliging de belangen van het kind zouden worden verwaarloosd.

Artikel 253c
1. De tot het gezag bevoegde vader van het kind, die nimmer het gezag gezamenlijk met de moeder heeft uitgeoefend, kan de rechtbank verzoeken hem met het gezag over het kind te belasten.
2. Wanneer de moeder het gezag over het kind uitoefent, wordt dit verzoek slechts ingewilligd, indien de rechter dit in het belang van het kind wenselijk oordeelt.
3. Wanneer niet in het gezag is voorzien of wanneer een voogd het gezag uitoefent, wordt het verzoek slechts afgewezen, indien gegronde vrees bestaat dat bij inwilliging de belangen van het kind zouden worden verwaarloosd.

Artikel 253d
1. Indien de voorziening in het gezag over een kind als bedoeld in artikel 253b, eerste lid, van dit boek komt te ontbreken, kunnen zowel zijn moeder als zijn vader dan wel beiden voor zover zij tot het gezag bevoegd zijn—de rechtbank verzoeken met het gezag onderscheidenlijk gezamenlijk gezag te worden belast.
2. Het in het eerste lid bedoelde verzoek wordt slechts afgewezen, indien gegronde vrees bestaat dat bij inwilliging de belangen van het kind zouden worden verwaarloosd.
3. Hebben beiden een verzoek ingediend anders dan tot gezamenlijke gezagsuitoefening, dan willigt de rechter het verzoek in van degene wiens gezag over het kind hij het meeste in het belang van het kind oordeelt.
4. Indien, voordat over het verzoek van één ouder is beslist, de andere ouder van rechtswege het gezag over het kind verkrijgt, willigt de rechter het verzoek slechts in, indien hij dit in het belang van het kind wenselijk oordeelt.
[...]

Artikel 254
1 Indien een minderjarige zodanig opgroeit, dat zijn zedelijke of geestelijke belangen of zijn gezondheid ernstig worden bedreigd, en andere middelen ter afwending van deze bedreiging hebben gefaald of, naar is te voorzien, zullen falen, kan de kinderrechter hem onder toezicht stellen van een stichting als bedoeld in artikel 1, onder f, van de Wet op de jeugdzorg.

2 De kinderrechter kan een in het eerste lid bedoelde minderjarige door of voor wie een aanvraag tot het verlenen van een verblijfsvergunning voor bepaalde tijd als bedoeld in artikel 28 van de Vreemdelingenwet 2000 is ingediend en die in verband daarmee in een opvangcentrum als bedoeld in artikel 1, onder d, van de Wet Centraal Orgaan opvang asielzoekers verblijft, onder toezicht stellen van een daartoe door Onze Minister van Justitie aanvaarde rechtspersoon.
3 Onze Minister van Justitie kan voorwaarden stellen bij of voorschriften verbinden aan de aanvaarding, bedoeld in het tweede lid, en de rechtspersoon voor een bepaalde tijd aanvaarden.
4 De kinderrechter kan een minderjarige onder toezicht stellen op verzoek van een ouder, een ander die de minderjarige als behorende tot zijn gezin verzorgt en opvoedt, de raad voor de kinderbescherming, of het openbaar ministerie.
5 Op verzoek van de stichting, dan wel op verzoek van de met het gezag belaste ouder of de minderjarige van twaalf jaren of ouder, kan de kinderrechter de stichting, bedoeld in artikel 1, onder f, van de Wet op de jeugdzorg, die het toezicht heeft, vervangen door een zodanige stichting in een andere provincie. De raad voor de kinderbescherming is bevoegd het in de vorige volzin bedoelde verzoek in te dienen, indien de raad van oordeel blijft dat de uithuisplaatsing niet op de voet van artikel 263, eerste lid, dient te worden beëindigd. Indien ten tijde van een verlenging van de duur van de ondertoezichtstelling niet meer wordt voldaan aan de eisen voor benoembaarheid, bedoeld in het tweede lid, vervangt de kinderrechter ambtshalve de door Onze Minister van Justitie aanvaarde rechtspersoon door een stichting als bedoeld in artikel 1, onder f, van de Wet op de jeugdzorg, tenzij voortzetting van de taken door bedoelde rechtspersoon hem om reden van continuïteit noodzakelijk voorkomt.
6 Op een rechtspersoon als bedoeld in het tweede lid, zijn de bepalingen van de afdelingen 4 en 5 alsmede artikel 326 van overeenkomstige toepassing. In geval van vervanging op de voet van het vijfde lid van de in het tweede lid bedoelde rechtspersoon, wordt de stichting, bedoeld in artikel 1, onder f, van de Wet op de jeugdzorg in de provincie waar de desbetreffende minderjarige duurzaam verblijft benoemd.

Artikel 255
De kinderrechter kan hangende het onderzoek de minderjarige voorlopig onder toezicht stellen indien dit dringend en onverwijld noodzakelijk is. Hij bepaalt de duur van dit voorlopige toezicht op ten hoogste drie maanden en kan de beslissing te allen tijde herroepen.

Jurisprudence

Case 1

Male circumcision involves irreversible physical consequences and pain, but cannot be recognised as malicious wounding. The decision concerning male circumcision of a minor can only be made by his parents (with recognised parental authority) or legal guardians. (Parket bij de Hoge Raad, 5 July 2011, ECLI:NL:PHR:2011:BQ6690)[19]

Case 2

The Court adjudicated in the case of a runaway Moroccan girl (a minor), who did not want to obey the Islamic rules and norms followed by her parents (both of Moroccan origin). The Court held that the right to educate children in accordance with parents' (Islamic) religious rules, beliefs and culture cannot restrict the rights and freedoms of others (i.e. the children). According to the Court, in cases when the necessary measures are required in order to protect a minor, Dutch national family law may be applied, even if such provisions do not conform to the system of law valid in the parents' country of origin (i.e. Moroccan-Islamic law). This concerns e.g. parental authority, which may thereby be limited. (Hoge Raad, 1 July 1982, NJ 1983, 201)

19 Available at http://uitspraken.rechtspraak.nl/inziendocument?id=ECLI:NL:PHR:2011:BQ6690 [last accessed on 10 March 2014].

Bibliography

Aerts, Monique C.M., *Sociaal recht. De zelfstandige in het sociaal recht* (Amsterdam: Kluwer, 2007).

Berger, Maurits, 'Sharia in Nederland is vaak keurig Nederlands', *Mens en Maatschappij*, 56 (2007), pp. 506–510.

Bernts, Tom, Gert de Jong and Hasan Yar, 'Een religieuze atlas van Nederland' in *Geloven in het publieke domein. Verkenningen van een dubbele transformatie*, Wim B.H.J. van de Donk, Petra Jonkers, Gerrit J. Kronjee, Rob J.J.M. Plum (eds.) (Amsterdam: Amsterdam University Press, 2006).

Bijsterveld, Sophie C. van, *Godsdienstvrijheid in Europees perspectief* (Deventer: W.E.J. Tjeenk Willink, 1998).

Bijsterveld, Sophie C. van, 'Państwo i kościół w Holandii' in *Państwo i kościół w krajach Unii Europejskiej*, Gerhard Robbers (ed.) (Wrocław: Kolonia Limited, 2007).

Boender, Welmoet, *Imam in Nederland. Opvattingen over zijn religieuze rol in de samenleving* (Amsterdam: Bert Bakker, 2007).

Boer, Jan de, *Personen- en familierecht*, 8th edition (Deventer: Kluwer, 2010).

Bok, A.J., *Subsidies*, Mon. Awb A6, (Gouda: Kluwer, 2002).

Brand, Charlotte, '"Moorse minaretten" op kosten van de staat?' in *Jaarboek Parlementaire Geschiedenis 2005. God in de Nederlandse Politiek*, Carla van Baalen, Anne Bos, Willen Breedveld, Peter van der Heiden, Jan Ramakers, Ineke Secker (Den Haag: Sdu Uitgevers, 2005).

Davelaar, Maarten and Eliane Smits van Waesberghe, *Tussen principes en pragmatisme. Een onderzoek onder Nederlandse gemeenten naar de subsidiëring van levensbeschouwelijke organisaties* (Utrecht: FORUM, Instituut voor Multiculturele Vraagstukken, 2010).

Dekker van Bijsterveld, Sophie C. den, *De verhouding tussen kerk en staat in het licht van de grondrechten* (Zwolle: W.E.J. Tjeenk Willink, 1988).

Douwes, Dick, Martijn de Koning and Welmoet Boender, *Nederlandse moslims: van migrant tot burger* (Amsterdam: Amsterdam University Press—Salomé, 2005).

Fluiten, Pieter S. and Wijnand A. Zondag, 'Godsdienst in arbeidsverhoudingen', *Tijdschrift voor arbeid en sociale zekerheid*, SMA 11/12 (2007) (Deventer: Kluwer, 2007).

Gerards, Janneke H., 'Botsende grondrechten, het gelijkheidsbeginsel en belangenafwegingen door de rechter', in *Moderne gelijkheid. Lezingen, gehouden tijdens de Rechten van de mens-dag van de Erasmus Universiteit Rotterdam op 10 december 2004*, Janneke H. Gerards, Siep Stuurman, (Den Haag: Boom Juridische Uitgevers, 2005).

Heuts, Lars, Jeanine Klaver, Inge van der Welle and Timke Visser, *Evaluatie Islam- en Imamopleidingen in Nederland*, Eindrapport (Amsterdam: Regioplan Beleidsonderzoek, 2012).

Hooven ten, Marcel, 'Religie verdeelt Nederland' in *Ongewenste goden. De publieke rol van religie in Nederland,* Marcel ten Hooven, Theo de Wit (eds.) (Amsterdam: SUN, 2006).

Janssens, Alfred L.J. and Aernout J. Nieuwenhuis, *Uitingsdelicten* (Deventer: Kluwer, 2005).

Koning, Martijn de, 'Netherlands' in *Yearbook of Muslims in Europe*, vol. 1, Jørgen S. Nielsen, Samim Akgönül, Ahmet Alibašić, Brigitte Maréchal, Christian Moe (eds.) (Leiden: Brill, 2009).

Labuschagne, Barend Christoffel, *Godsdienstvrijheid en niet-gevestigde religies. Een grondrechtelijk-rechtsfilosofische studie naar de betekenis en grenzen van religieuze tolerantie* (Groningen: Wolters-Noordhoff, 1994)

Landman, Nico, 'Kerkgenootschap, stichting of vereniging: De juridische structuur van islamitische organisaties in Nederland' in *Recht van de Islam 8*, Susan W.E. Rutten (ed.) (Maastricht: RIMO, 1990), available at http://www.verenigingrimo.nl/wp/wp-content/uploads/recht8_landman.pdf.

Loenen, Titia, *Geloof in het geding: juridische grenzen van religieus pluralisme in het perspectief van de mensenrechten* (Den Haag: SDU, 2006).

Nieuwenhuis, Aernout J., *Over de grens van de vrijheid van meningsuiting* (Nijmegen: Ars Aequi Libri, 2006).

Oldenhuis, Fokko, Jan G. Brouwer, Dana N.R. Wegerif and Fabian E. Keijzer, *Schurende relaties tussen recht en religie* (Assen: Van Gorcum, 2007).

Pot, Combertus W. van der, *Handboek van het Nederlandse staatsrecht*, 15th edition (Deventer: Kluwer, 2006).

Potz, Richard, and Wolfgang Wieshaider (eds.), *Islam and the European Union* (Leuven: Peeters, 2004).

Potz, Richard and Wolfgang Wieshaider, 'Religious Entities as Legal Persons—Parts of Western and Central Europe (Belgium, Germany, Ireland, Luxemburg, The Netherlands, Austria, The United Kingdom of Great Britain and Northern Ireland)' in Lars Friedner (ed.), *Churches and Other Religious Organisations and Legal Persons*, European Consortium for Church-State Research. Conference (Leuven: Peeters, 2007).

Rath, Jan, Rinus Penninx, Kees Groenendijk and Astrid Meijer, *Nederland en zijn Islam. Een ontzuilende samenleving reageert op het onstaat van een geloofgemeenschap* (Amsterdam: Het Spinhuis, 1996).

Rynkowski, Michał, 'Remarks on Art. I-52 of the Constitutional Treaty: New Aspects of the European Ecclesiastical Law?', *German Law Journal*, 11 (2005).

Sauer, Birgit, 'Headscarf regimes in Europe: Diversity Policies at the intersection of gender, culture and religion', *Comparative European Politics*, 7 (2009), pp. 75–94.

Shadid, Wasif A.R. and Peter S. van Koningsveld (eds.), *Islam in Dutch Society: Current Developments and Future Prospects*, (Kampen: Kok, 1992).

Shadid, Wasif A.R. and Peter S. van Koningsveld, *Islam in Nederland en België. Religieuze institutionalisering in twee landen met een gemeenschappelijke voorgeschiedenis*, (Leuven: Peeters, 2008).

Strijen, Cees R. van, *Lexplicatie: De complete wetgeving toegelicht: Wet op de Lijkbezorging* (Deventer: Kluwer, 2009).

Sunier, Thijl, 'Islam in the Netherlands. A nation despite religious communities?', in *Religious Newcomers and the Nation State. Political Culture and Organized Religion in France and the Netherlands*, Erik Sengers, Thijl Sunier (eds.) (Delft: Eburon, 2010), pp. 115–130.

Sunier, Thijl, 'Moslims in de Nederlandse politieke arena', in *Emancipatie en subcultuur. Sociale bewegingen in België en Nederland*, Thijl Sunier, Jan Willem Duijvendak, Sawitri Saharso, Fridus Steijlen (eds.) (Amsterdam: Instituut voor Publiek en Politiek, 2000).

Vellenga, Sipco, Sadik Harchaoui, Halim El Madkouri and Baukje Sijses, *Mist in de polder. Zicht op ontwikkelingen omtrent de islam in Nederland* (Amsterdam: Aksant, 2009).

Vermeulen, Ben (ed.), *Overwegingen bij een boerka verbod. Zienswijze van de deskundigen inzake een verbod op gezichtsbedekkende kleding* (The Hague, 2006), available at https://openaccess.leidenuniv.nl/bitstream/handle/1887/13377/7%20niqab_rapport.pdf?sequence=1.

Wal, Peterjan van der, and Mariëlle Cuijpers, *Financiering van geestelijke verzorging voor ouderen. Mogelijkheden voor de verbreding van het werkterrein en de inzet van geestelijk verzorgers*, Vilans/Expertisenetwerk Levensvragen en Ouderen (Utrecht 2012), available at http://www.vilans.nl/docs/producten/fingeestverzorgouderendef.pdf

Zdanowski, Jerzy, 'Muzułmanie w Holandii' in *Muzułmanie w Europie*, Anna Parzymies (ed.) (Warszawa: DIALOG, 2005).

Internet Sources

www.cbs.nl
www.cgb.nl
www.cmoweb.nl
www.eerstekamer.nl
www.gvoenhvo.nl
www.mensenrechten.nl
www.ntkr.nl
www.nvao.net
www.onderwijsinspectie.nl
www.onderwijsraad.nl

www.radar.nl
www.rijksoverheid.nl
www.rechtspraak.nl
www.wetboek-online.nl
www.wetten.overheid.nl

Index